A MAIDAN VIEW

The Magic of Indian Cricket

A MAIDAN VIEW

The Magic of Indian Cricket

Mihir Bose

London
GEORGE ALLEN & UNWIN
Boston   Sydney

**George Allen & Unwin (Publishers) Ltd,
40 Museum Street, London WC1A 1LU, UK**

George Allen & Unwin (Publishers) Ltd,
Park Lane, Hemel Hempstead, Herts HP2 4TE, UK

Allen & Unwin Inc.,
8 Winchester Place, Winchester, Mass 01890, USA

George Allen & Unwin Australia Pty Ltd,
8 Napier Street, North Sydney, NSW 2060, Australia

George Allen & Unwin with the
Port Nicholson Press
PO Box 11-838 Wellington, New Zealand

First published in 1986

British Library Cataloguing in Publication Data

Bose, Mihir
A maidan view: the magic of Indian cricket.
1. Cricket – India – History
I. Title
796.35′865   GV928.I4

ISBN 0–04–796119–8

Set in 11½ on 13 point Garamond by
Nene Phototypesetters Ltd, Northampton
and printed in Great Britain
by Butler & Tanner Ltd, Frome and London

To Janet and Yehuda
For encouraging those non-cricketing things in me
that also form part of this book.

CONTENTS

ACKNOWLEDGEMENTS

This book has a most curious history. It started as a biography, it has ended up as something of a history of modern India.

Some years ago I wrote a biography of Keith Miller for George Allen & Unwin. It did not, as I had fantasised, make my fortune – none of my books have – but my publishers were pleased and suggested that I write another book. We eventually settled on a biography of Ranji. I was half way through the book when we learned that Alan Ross was about to publish his biography of Ranji. The project was abandoned and it was then that an idea of a book on Indian cricket which would look beyond the hype and the mystique suggested itself. I am grateful to John Newth for encouraging the idea and to Derek Wyatt for mixing the carrots and sticks in the right proportion to induce me to come up with the goods. This book has been more trouble than most of my other books, but it has also been more fun – Derek was responsible for both the trouble and the fun.

I am also grateful to John Lovesey and David Robson, successive Sports Editors of the *Sunday Times*, for the help and encouragement they have given me over the years. John was brave enough to hire me, and David has overcome his natural Yorkshire belief that God, if not like Boycott, is at least a Yorkshireman. They have allowed me to inflict myself on the *Sunday Times* readers. I have learnt much from Nick Mason and Jim Pegg, both about journalism and cricket. Both of us have a partiality for fish, though Jim being the sort of pragmatic chap he is would no doubt rubbish Jeeves' idea that eating fish improves the brain power.

Paul Barker of *New Society* and Jerome Burne and Don Atyeo of *Time Out*, together with Gilliam Greenwood, former Editor of the *Literary Review*, and Sharad Kotnis of *Sportsweek*, have all encouraged me by publishing ideas and views on Indian cricket which form the basis of this book. As has Vinod Mehta, editor of the *Bombay Sunday Observer*.

Many friends in India and England have, over the years, sustained – or suffered – my constant discourses on cricket, and particularly Indian cricket. Some like Edwin, Bala and Hubert feature in this book; others like Munir and Ramesh remain good friends proving distance need not always sever childhood ties. English friends, even those indifferent to cricket, have indulged my favourite preoccupation. Cricket, particularly club cricket, has introduced me to a circle of friends I would never have otherwise met and I am grateful to all of them.

David Smith, Nigel Dudley, Bruce Parey and Garth Hewitt have encouraged my fantasies of the cricketer and cricket writer, Deborah Harman – despite the appalling hereditary handicap of being born into an Arsenal-supporting family – has been marvellously helpful and Mark and Rose Streatfeild, in their very different ways, have been just as efficient as Derek Wyatt in chiding me about the tardy progress of this book.

My parents and their friends indulged their love for the game and without the large retinue of servants and staff that my father employed, I would certainly not have been introduced to maidan cricket the way I was. I thank them and my sisters Tripti and Pavna, for their patience and understanding, and to my father's staff for their co-operation. In particular, Shankar, Arjun and Mr Kandalgoakar, who was given time off by my father to escort me to Test Matches. As ever, Sue Cairncross proved a model secretary despite the almost impossible demands I sometimes made on her.

Above all I owe the greatest debt of gratitude to Indian cricket and its cricketers. My earliest memory of Test cricket is being taken to the house of a friend of my mother's whose verandah conveniently overlooked the Brabourne Stadium. Checking through Wisden I can now actually place the date. It was 15 December 1951, the second day of the second Test Match between India and England. As I recall, we were meant to watch Hazare grind England to dust. But in trying to hook a short pitched ball from Ridgeway he played it onto his forehead, cutting it badly. Wisden says that 'not only did that affect his batting in the match, but he seemed to lose all confidence and was never the same player in the three remaining Tests'. All that history has come later. I was four then, but I can still recall the surprise and anguish felt on the balcony as Hazare retired. Since then Indian cricket has often surprised me, caused me a great deal of anguish but also provided moments of great joy. This book, although it may not read like that, is meant to repay some of the enjoyment I have had from Indian cricket.

Mihir Bose
London, 1986

CHAPTER 1

India – Whose India?

Sometime in the 1930s Jawaharlal Nehru, independent India's first Prime Minister and father of Indira Gandhi, was addressing a large political gathering. He was then leading the Indians in their epic fight against British rule and as he spoke that day, like so often before, the crowd shouted 'Bharat Mata ki jai' (Long Live Mother India). It was the common political greeting of Indian crowds and Nehru had heard it often. But that day, as the cry was raised, he stopped speaking and, pointing to the crowd, asked 'What is Mother India? What does it mean to you?'

The crowd were mystified. They were not used to their political leaders asking them questions but Nehru insisted on a reply and, slowly, some of them pointed to the ground to indicate that was Mother India. Nehru interrupted them with that mixture of impatience and hautiness that so characterised him and told his audience that if Mother India, which they were wishing a long life meant anything, it meant them, not the earth. 'It is you, all of you together, you are India.' The crowd cheered ever more lustily and the incident was to become famous – almost every Nehru biographer has narrated it. In later years Nehru himself would make that impromptu question and answer session part of his unique method of arousing and educating an Indian crowd.

But if Nehru scored an important, populist point, the question 'What is India, what does it represent?' is not easily answered. India is as confusing to Indians themselves as it is to foreigners. Even the name India is not something given by Indians. The Persians and the Greeks, trying to define the people who lived along the river Sindhu, tumbled on the words Indian and Hindu. The word Sindhu, a Sanskrit word, seemed too much for the ancient Persians and Greeks. They corrupted it to Indus – which is what the great river of the Punjab is called – and then trying to define the inhabitants 'of the region of the river Indus' the Persian and Greek tongues diverged. The Persian word was aspirated and came out as Hindu, the Greek one was softly breathed and came out as India. In the curious, convoluted way Indian history was made, India came to stand for the subcontinent beyond the Indus

1

bounded by the Himalayas, while Hindu became the word used to define the religion of the people who inhabited the region.

Many centuries later the Orientalists discovering India added another twist. They discovered the Hindus had no name for their religion. Hindus knew it – and still know it – as Sanatana Dharma – the Eternal way. Orientalists coined the term Hinduism to describe the complex beliefs that underpinned the religion. As Nirad Chaudhuri has pointed out, on that analogy, the Greek religion might be called Hellenism or even Graecism. The Orientalists could hardly have realised the consequences of their actions. In modern India the word Indian represents all Indians of whatever religion. The country is secular, every religious group has full religious and political rights and Mohammed Azharuddin would be most upset if you called him a Hindu. He is a Muslim and an Indian.

This probably explains why, nearly forty years after the British withdrew from India, Indians still find it necessary to refight the old colonial wars with the British. The British, in seeking to justify their imperialism, asserted that India was not a nation that they, the British, had unified India. Once they left, India would break up. In fact the withdrawal of the British saw the country partitioned between India and Pakistan. During the struggle with the Raj, Indian nationalists rebutted the British arguments by stressing the pre-British greatness of India and, perhaps under-standably, overegging their arguments by waxing eloquently about a land of milk and honey in which there had been no problems, no caste system and no evils, only genuine Indian harmony and peace. A state of bliss ruined by British rule. To balance the British presentation of the Raj in heroic, almost Roman, terms (the British were rather fond of comparing their Empire to the Roman one) the Indian nationalists wrote books such as that by K. M. Munishi whose title *The Ruin that Britain Wrought* made its message plain.

Today, as a new generation of right-wing British historians seeks to justify the Empire in terms of historical necessity and inevitability – borrowing, curiously, from Karl Marx who had much the same ideas – Indians find it necessary to reassert the country's historical continuity. Thus Indian journalist M. J. Akbar devotes a good deal of his book *India: The Seige Within* (Penguin, 1985) to answer British charges that the imperial power unified India:

2

The British took Delhi in 1857; the Indian National Congress was born in 1885. It must have been an extraordinary rule which in just three decades managed to integrate a territory as large as this subcontinent whose parts had, it seems, 'nothing in common' for thousands of years. Two hundred and fifty years before Christ, Ashoka's administration took Buddhism into every corner of India, but apparently did not leave any sense of common identity. Brihaspati's principles of natural justice have been a part of popular faith for centuries, but it is the British courts which allegedly gave India a sense of law. The Mughal emperor Akbar's administrative structures held together his vast empire in the sixteenth century, but we must believe that it is the British Collector in the district who taught Indians how to rule themselves. Shankara walked from Kerala to Kashmir to preach Hinduism before William of Normandy reached Britain, but it is the British railways which united India through a communications network! The argument of unity by courtesy of the British empire falls on many counts, but the simplest is that even in 1947 nearly half of this country was not ruled by the British but by their native allies, who employed Indian administrators. School maps did show the whole of India painted red, but the princely states were not technically a part of British India. A separate accession treaty had to be obtained from each one of the 565 princely states on this subcontinent at the time of independence.

To many Indians, particularly to my generation, which is also that of Salman Rushdie's midnight children, the subcontinent's division between India, Pakistan and now Bangladesh is the fault of the British policy of divide and rule. Many would echo the Indian politician Mohammed Ali's charge, as made to Lord Sankey at the first round-table conference in London in November 1930. 'My Lord, divide and rule is the order of the day. But in India we divide and you rule'.

After the assassination of Mrs Gandhi and the fearsome anti-Sikh riots that swept Delhi, Indians, both in India and in this country, felt outraged by questions in the British media about whether India would survive. This merely confirmed their suspicions about Western machinations to undermine Indian independence. Mrs Gandhi had often campaigned on the slogan of 'the foreign hand' seeking to undermine India, and significantly

3

her successor and son, Rajiv Gandhi, skilfully used the fear of the country disintegrating if the people did not vote for his Congress Party to secure a massive majority just two months after his mother's death. Many Indians genuinely believe that Sikh extremism which finally culminated in Mrs Gandhi's death has been tolerated if not abetted by the West and recent years have seen protests against the BBC for allowing Sikh extremists to voice their anti-Indian sentiments.

Individual Britons did love India, even Indians, but they did not confuse this with their loyalty to their own country. The only paradise viceroys promoted was Great Britain and educated Indians, taking their cue from the British in India, often referred to Britain as 'home', though many never saw the place and only knew it as an exotic land which supplied the sahibs (Indian word for Englishmen) and memsahibs (the English female) who ruled their country. For Indians of my generation England as home does have a sardonic touch. This is particularly so when returning to this country we are welcomed by immigration officers who say, with just a touch of sneer in their voice, 'Welcome home', pause, 'Sir'. But for at least one group of Indians, the Anglo-Indians – the unfortunate racial products of the short-lived and fairly disastrous racial mixing of Indians and English – home is still real, and some of them build elaborate fantasies about 'going home' only to have them shattered by the hard-faced British consular staff in India.

The clash between the two insular traditions came early in the Indo-British contact though with different results – for both. The Asian insularity shoring up a dying civilisation, the British one actually helping strengthen a vigorous, acquisitive seventeenth- and eighteenth-century culture. When the British first began to travel to India, both Indian and Western civilisations were at about the same stage of material development. If anything the court of Jehangir – to whom the British petitioned to be allowed to trade – was much more resplendent that that of his contemporary, Elizabeth I. But whereas Elizabeth encouraged the British expansion overseas, Jehangir's court, for all its wealth and power, had lapsed into the form of Indian chauvinism that had so enraged Alberuni, the first and probably the greatest Muslim scholar to study India and the Hindus. 'The Hindus believe that there is no country but theirs, no nation like theirs, no kings like theirs, no religion like theirs, no science like theirs. They are haughty, foolishly vain, self-conceited.' As Nirad Chaudhuri has said 'this

4

megalomania became far more intense and unshakable under Muslim rule, and remained a living passion under British rule'.

The British did seek to temper it by not only extolling their own paradise home but by educating a class of Indians who, in Macaulay's famous minute of 1833, much quoted, much misunderstood, would be English in everything – thoughts, ideas, dress, feel – except for the colour of their skin. But Macaulay's ambitions were limited – he saw the creation of an élite that would help the British rule India, not the cultural conversion of all Indians. Even this limited ambition was far removed from the 'La Mission civilisatrice de la France en Orient' that characterised the French Empire. Most British administrators shuddered at such thoughts and, distrustful of culture as they were, placed greater emphasis on a good administration and a stable government.

The contrast in British and French attitudes was well brought out by Percy Loraine, one of the great Foreign Office mandarins of the interwar period when he spoke of 'our illogical Imperial story'. In India the illogicality meant that the Indian products of English-style universities were disowned by the very British who had created their universities. It was and remains the greatest infanticide in intellectual history, disowning not your blood-children, but your own intellectual progeny.

As the Indians emerged from these English-style universities, reared on John Stuart Mill, the British denounced them as dangerous radicals who did not understand their own country-men. Lord Curzon railed against the monstrous army of infernal lawyers that the British had created in India and reserved a special scorn for the British-educated Indian. A scorn that was most vividly expressed by Sir Reginald Craddock who spoke for much of the Raj when he said, 'We British who have served India are accused of lack of sympathy. But with whom should we sympathise the most? With the millions who are poor and helpless or with the few who have always exploited them? . . . The intelligentsia of a country should be the voice expressing the thoughts of the people, which they can understand even though they might not so well express themselves. This is not so in India. The language the intellectuals speak is not understood by the people.'

The British having played their part in 'denationalising' the Indian élite, now asserted that they were the true heirs to the Moghul empires and other Indian empires and best understood the oppressed millions of Indians. Hardly·surprising that the

Indian élite took a somewhat different view and saw the British assertion as an easy justification for its rule.

Nowhere was this complex British response to India more evident than in Bengal. Bengal, in eastern India, was the first province to fall to the British, the Bengalis the first to realise the usefulness of adapting to their new rules. So energetic and imaginative was their response that it was to lead to a remarkable nineteenth-century renaissance – a time of iconoclasm, a time of change, a time when the decadent, dying Indian culture suddenly confronted with a vibrant, confident Western one, revived in splendid style. It was to lead to the flowering of Bengali literature, a whole series of poets and writers culminating in Tagore, who became the first – and so far the only – Indian to win the Nobel prize in literature. The most vivid modern product of this Indo-British honeymoon is Satyajit Ray, India's greatest film director and very much part of the liberal-humanist Western tradition.

Yet, in both the British and the Bengalis, rulers and ruled this resulted only in hate and scorn. In *The Lost Hero,* my biography of Subhas Bose, the Indian nationalist, I discussed this aspect of the Indo-British connection:

> The early British scorned the Bengalis for the ease with which they had allowed Clive and his East India Company men to conquer them. The later Imperial Raj ridiculed their efforts to imbibe English culture and education. In the eighteenth century Luke Scrafton could write of the Bengalis as a 'slightly made people' with 'dejected minds' that 'fall an easy prey to every invader': by the time Kipling arrived the Bengali *babu* proudly flaunting his 'BA failed' and claiming acquaintance with Shakespeare, was a finely honed figure of Raj fun. No other great empire – not the Roman, or even the Russian – had been so horrified at the thought of cultural proselytisation.
>
> Malcolm Muggeridge has suggested that Arabs have always had a great appeal for a certain type of upper-class Englishman; partly, perhaps, because they are given to sodomy – a favourite pursuit at English boarding schools – but in any case because they have a seeming simplicity of character and directness of manner which, in the days of the British Raj and the Palestine Mandate, contrasted agreeably with the deviousness of the Indian Hindus and the Israeli Jews. Even allowing for

Muggeridge's characteristic reference to sodomy, a certain latent anti-Semitism did co-exist with promotion of Muslims and virulent Hindu-baiting. Quite soon after the Raj had been established, Indians were divided between, on the one hand, the ugly, deceitful Bengalis who, finding the Raj's liberal education inadequate, created the first nationalist movement; and, on the other hand, the good Indians: the tall, upright, uncomplicated martial races of the North, who were credited with a certain Indian version of public-schoolboy comradeship and trust. Some of this reflected the fact that the North Indians had given the British a tough time as they tried to conquer India. Conveniently, they were also conservative – even obscurantist – and hostile to progressive Western ideas. This suited the Raj's purpose admirably.

It was an amazing contradiction. Marx had suggested that the Raj would be an unwitting 'tool of history'. If its administration was oppressive, the import of modern Western ideas would break open the hermetically sealed Asian village communities and make them part of the world historical mainstream. Instead the British relied on the hermetically sealed Indian communities and kingdoms to maintain their rule in India. This was not merely good imperial politics, it was a geographical must. It arose from the curious way the British acquired their Empire. For though we speak of the British ruling India for nearly 200 years, from Clive's conquest of Bengal in 1757 to Mountbatten's withdrawal in 1947, there was no formal conquest of India as there was of the Incas by Spain – and even in 1947 the British only really controlled just over half the country.

Nor in fact was Clive's conquest of Bengal the sort of thing that would normally be defined as a conquest. Superficially the Battle of Plassey, in which he defeated Bengal's King Siraj-ud-daullah, was like an early version of a one-day cricket international with the dare-devilry of Clive's cavalry winning the day, after rain had affected Siraj's powder. But in reality the match had been 'fixed'. Clive had bribed Mir-Jaffar, Siraj's ambitious Commander-in-Chief promising him the kingship of Bengal in exchange for remaining neutral and the result of the battle was Mir-Jaffar replacing Siraj on the throne of Bengal and Clive and his men earning a lot of money.

For the next ninety years as the Mughal Empire continued to collapse – its collapse had triggered the eighteenth-century chaos and anarchy in India and provided Clive his platform – the British continued their 'conquests'. Again not India versus Britain but Indians versus Indians, with the British siding once with this lot of Indians, once with another. This is not to deny the divisions, greed, worthlessness and sheer political and military incompetence of the Indian feudal leadership. Divided by religion, caste, communal and almost every other consideration most of them seem to be motivated by greed, and many of them did not know what they were fighting for, or even acknowledged themselves as Indians. Nor can one doubt the military and political genius of Clive and his successors. But the important point to note is that the British did not conquer India as the Germans rolled over Europe in the Second World War. The British way was of making and unmaking Indian feudal kings and garnering more power and money for themselves.

Most of the troops the British controlled in India were actually Indians and they fought not under the banner of the British government, but the East India Company which had been granted a charter to trade in India by Elizabeth I. In fact many of the conquests between 1757 and 1857 were freelance efforts by officials of the East India Company ignoring, or even disobeying the orders of their head office in London. India's fabled riches had first attracted the British to India and in the chaos of the eighteenth century, the British in India saw a splendid opportunity to make their own private fortunes and promptly and shrewdly made the most of the opportunity.

So curious was the nature of the British conquest that even in May 1857 – just a month before the centenary of the Battle of Plassey – a Mughal emperor still ruled in Delhi and the British still paid homage to him. It was a piece of elaborate fiction, but instructive at that. As the British had mopped up the Indian feudal powers, banishing some, pensioning others, they did so almost as agents of the 'great Mughal' in Delhi. It was the most curious form of political leasehold tenancy. After every battle the Mughal Emperor would grant the British 'firmans' – rights – to levy taxes and control a territory and, in theory, the British still accepted the Mughal Emperor as ruler of India – and the ultimate freeholder of the country. Four times a year they presented themselves to the Emperor and offered him *nazar* – tribute.

This fiction ended in May 1857 when the Indian troops of the East India Company, who had provided the fighting muscle for the

8

British in the past century, mutinied. The troops rushed to Delhi and sought to make Bahadur Shah a real emperor again. He, a fantasist hovering perhaps between the status of gnat and fly, tried to shoo them away saying he was a mere pensioner and if it was more money they wanted, they should go to the British. But something of the old ancestral Mughal blood must have stirred in this pathetic fantasist's veins for he did eventually lead, and for a short time the pensioner became a real emperor.

In some ways this, at last, provided an India versus British contest. But here again the lines were confused. Many of the Indians, being educated in the Macaulay-inspired universities, sided with the British and saw the revolt as the last throw of the old Indian feudal order. More crucially, in the vital northern Indian plains where Indian troops heavily outnumbered the British by six to one, three crucial elements: Sikhs, Hindu Gurkhas and Punjabi Muslims, seeing in this opportunities to recoup some of their earlier losses sided with the British.

In September 1857 the British conquered Delhi and did it in a style that the previous conquerors of the Indian capital would have recognised. Bahadur Shah was banished to Rangoon, three of his sons murdered, several others summarily shot, and almost every male inhabitant of Delhi considered guilty of treachery and betrayal. Inflamed by the revolt – and reports of Indian cruelty – much of it exaggerated – the British and their Indian allies extracted terrible vengeance. Mutineers were shot from cannons – hanging was almost a mercy – soldiers and officers looted so thoroughly that almost everyone of them could have retired, and many did, and the Urdu poet Ghalib wrote of the 'vast ocean of blood before me' as he surveyed a British-conquered Delhi. Interestingly, while William Howard Russell of *The Times* was shocked by the brutality of the British, he freely took part in the looting regretting that he could not, as at Lucknow, take full advantage of his chances.

Now, for the first time, India formally passed to the British government and Queen Victoria became Empress of India. Even then the prerevolt tenancy agreements remained. Five hundred and sixty-five Indian kingdoms had treaty arrangements with the British Crown which allowed the rulers complete autonomy in their own kingdom – save the presence of a British resident – and with the British in charge of their foreign relations. After 1857 the British ruled India in name and fact, but in these 565 kingdoms

9

nothing changed. Some of them were beneficially ruled like Baroda, others despotically like Kashmir or Hyderabad, but as long as the Indian King kept on the right side of the Viceroy, it did not matter. The mosaic of India that the British had inherited did not change. India remained a patchwork of feudal Indian-ruled states where the King was absolute monarch, and British provinces where Marx's unwitting tool of history set to work.

Yet it is a reflection of how slowly, if at all, the Marxist historical tool worked that even today the two peoples – Indians and British – have little or no understanding about each other. They even cannot agree on old historical facts. The first draft of my introduction to my biography of Subhas Bose, an Irish-style Indian nationalist, had to be toned down because it was felt that it would put off British reviewers who would consider it a bit too emotional and anti-British.

Since Bose sought to drive the British out of India through violent means, and I was writing a critical, but not an anti-Bose book, this criticism was strange. The British as conquerors naturally wrote the history books, for instance those on the Indian revolt, which stressed the Indian brutality and English heroism, while skating over the terrible British vengeance. Some years ago when I scripted a play that touched on the Indian revolt, an English member of the audience upset by the scenes of brutality, suggested to me that I had missed the point. 'Don't you think', he said, 'the English behaved like that in India because they were corrupted by Indian practices and habits'. I know what the modern Indian answer to that would be, though that evening I was rather shocked by the idea to come up with the right response. But even today Indians do feel the need to make a response and even M. J. Akbar, in an otherwise very perceptive analysis of modern India, cannot bring himself to admit that the British conquest of India was inevitable. The nationalists' argument that it was the result of Indian disunity and British machinations is vigorously argued – ignoring the political and military superiority that obviously underlay the British achievement. While Akbar rightly stresses, for instance, the excesses of the British during the Indian revolt, he feels it necessary to ignore the basic cruelty and intrigue that formed part of the Indian action.

Indians, like Akbar, products of independent India are often more anti-British than their parents. However, these modern

Indians, who would readily believe that British rule ruined India, do not extend their distrust in a personal fashion. The anti-British sentiments of this generation of Indians is restricted to its interpretation of the British role in India, not to ordinary Britons. I know of no visitor from Britain to India who has encountered any personal prejudice. As Indians often say, we hate what the Raj did, but not the individual Britons. One explanation for this, much favoured by Indians themselves, is that this dichotomy reflects the nature of the Indian independence struggle, particularly the ideas of Mahatma Gandhi. He often said that if the British became Indian he would have no objections to their staying in India. Partly it reflects the Indian ability – necessitated perhaps by the curious, often awful, nature of Indian history – to disassociate the individual from the institution. A dissonance necessary in order to understand India's historical pattern, or even survive. A dichotomy that can happily allow Indians to inherit and enjoy the institutions left behind by the Raj while seeking to make political capital from those Indians, like the communists, who sided with the British during the war when most nationalists were either neutral or anti-British.

A recent British visitor to India found concrete evidence of this Indian contradiction when attending the Calcutta Test in January 1985. The route from the hotel to Eden Gardens took him past two statues which seemed a bit baffling. One was of Subhas Bose, his right arm raised in a salute, and almost pointing to a column opposite him commemorating the Glorious Dead of the wars. During the Second World War Bose, as an extreme nationalist, joined with the Germans and Japanese and raised an army to drive the British out of India. The column of the Glorious Dead, first erected after the First World War, has names of Indians and English who fought and died for king and emperor during the two wars. To the visiting Englishman's eyes the two statues juxtaposed in that fashion, made no sense. Which of them represented India? Was Bose the hero and the Indians who fought for the British traitors? Or, as the British claimed, the other round?

The Indian answer is to stress Bose's patriotism, his love for his country, his secular nationalism, and skate over his possible fascist sympathies. Bose's early and mysterious death is mourned, or as Akbar puts it, it is India's loss that this 'great and completely secular nationalist . . . died too soon'. Bose is honoured on his

11

birthday, many of India's most prestigious streets are named after him and, periodically, there are rumours that he is alive and about to return to rescue India.

The Indians who fought in the British Indian army are ignored. In the Indian army barracks and histories, the achievements of these Indians are, of course, treasured and in that sense they are part of the modern Indian army's traditions. But outside the army little or nothing is known of the Indians who contributed in the First World War to Allenby's destruction of the Ottoman Empire, or in the Second to Montgomery's defeat of Rommel. During the First World War, Punch could print a cartoon of a turbanned Indian atop a horse saluting John Bull and saying, 'there are 165,000 of us, Sir, ready and waiting', modern Indians would rather not know – and even if they did it would make no sense. Certainly it is difficult to see any Indian film director wanting – or even able – to make a film comparable, say, to *Gallipoli* which honours the Australian achievement in the First World War.

Nations like individuals need to shut out awkward phases of their lives but the modern Indian tendency to do so has produced a country which is a strange mixture of sophistication and feudalism, neurosis and calm. An India which is eager for the latest gadgets from the West – during his 1984 election campaign, Rajiv Gandhi made much of the fact that he had installed a computer to help him in the elections – but distrusts the processes that produced the gadgets. An India which is eager to seek Western approbation – in fact finds it vitally necessary to help it make its own evaluation, but moans about any Western view that does not accord with its own. 'Why', ask many Indians, 'Why does the West hate us so', meaning why does it not give India more credit for its remarkable ability to make economic progress yet maintain democratic institutions.

As an Indian living in London and working for the British media – with whom the Indians have an extraordinary love/hate relationship – I am often subjected by my Indian friends in India to such dual pressures. 'Yes', they say, 'we know you have a good lifestyle in London. You earn a lot of money, living is good, telephones work, there is good entertainment, there is no pollution as in our cities, you have a wide choice of consumer goods. But wouldn't you really live in India? I mean, do you really like being a second-class citizen there, however well-fed?

Wouldn't you rather be a poorer, but first-class, citizen in your own country?'

The irony of such sentiments is that most of my Indian friends who make it probably have a higher standard of living than I do, they have servants, chauffeurs, quite a relaxed lifestyle and seem to be able to travel all round the world much more often than I do. To them I could only have been seduced by the West's riches – occasionally some have suggested I may have been seduced by the West's women as well. In their eyes India may be materially poor but it is spiritually rich. During the Raj this supposed spiritual richness of India compensated for the material prosperity of the West and helped Indians accept their colonial status. Since then as Westerners have travelled to India looking for gurus, Indians have triumphantly pointed to this as proof of India's superiority – in the spiritual department, 'the one that matters'. The West is seen as a material hulk with a pea of a spiritual brain. When I explain to my Indian friends that I live in the West because I find life here superior in almost every respect, many do not believe me, and at least one has felt that my remarks were 'traitorous' and indicated the corruption I had suffered. The modern Indian likes to visit the West, happily shops at Marks & Spencers, often keeps his scarce foreign exchange here, and desperately wants the West to treat India as a developed democracy but refuses to accept that the West has anything to offer except material rewards.

The modern Indian is not the only one with such views. The modern Arab tends to think the same way but, perhaps this is partly because the West, particularly the British, do still view India and Indians in a curious light which tells us more about the British and their ideas rather than the Indians.

For the British, India it was a distant world, part fantasy, part myth and always a puzzle seemingly just one clue away from solution, an India of legends whose spices had saved Rome from the fury of the fourth century Goths, or set Christopher Columbus on his adventures – full of glory but with such wretched maps that he readily confused America with India. A land that everybody searched for, yet nobody – not even Indians, perhaps, quite captured.

Had the British in India continued Warren Hastings's policy – and behaved very like the Muhgal rulers of India using Indians to help in their administration – the gap might have been bridged. But Hastings's departure, particularly its circumstances and the notorious trial in the House of Lords, created a breach between India and England, ruler and ruled, that was never healed. The British withdrew into their fastness with the Indian revolt accelerating this process and leading to a situation where for much of the Raj the British tried to remain above the battle and behave very like a super Hindu-caste which could not be infiltrated. Its outward manifestation was the creation of clubs and institutions where Indians, except as servants, were not allowed as members, its inner manifestation was a conception of 'our India' which nobody could challenge.

I was made most vividly aware of this early in 1984 when Thames screened the very popular *Jewel in the Crown,* a television adaptation of Paul Scott's *Raj Quartet.* I was concerned that the evident realism and attention to detail that had gone into *Jewel in the Crown* might make people believe that this was an accurate picture of India in the late 1940s.

I consider that the central starting point of *Jewel in the Crown* is wrong. Daphne Manners and Hari Kumar could never have met as they did, or even if they had, they could never have fallen in love. The English found the idea of inter-racial sex horrifying and the Indians did not much care for it either. As late as 1943 Leo Amery, then Secretary of State for India, would write to Lord Linlithgow, the Viceroy, expressing remorse that the British had not encouraged Indian princes to marry English women and produce a more virile race. Beautiful as *Jewel in the Crown* was, it sought to explain the Raj in terms of an English failure to mix with Indians – which was absurd and the whole series was pervaded by a pessimism that was historically ridiculous.

To say the least my English friends were surprised at my view, and as one put it, 'But that is how Paul Scott saw it. He was writing about the English in India, how can you as an Indian comment on how the English saw their India?' 'How the English saw their India', I think says it all. The real problem is that the British project their view of India as an objective view of India: they confuse their idea of India with India itself. When this India turns out to be not quite what they ordered, they are lost. It is the confusion my taxidriver felt early on the morning of Wednesday 31 October 1984, as Mrs Gandhi lay dying and I hurried to act as an Indian expert on the radio. 'I don't understand this', he said, gently shaking his head. 'When we were children the map of India used to be red and we always thought of it as one country. We didn't know about all these divisions: Hindus, Sikhs, Muslims. Where have they come from? Do you think we were right to leave the country? After all when we were there, there was no trouble was there?'

This confusion is not confined to politics and was reflected in cricket on the morning after England's 2–1 victory in the 1984–5 Test Series in India. *The Times* ran an article from its cricket correspondent under the headine, 'India's millions lost to the game they love'. The headline seemed to suggest that something had happened to turn Indians off the game. But that was not quite the thesis of John Woodcock:

> Of the male population of India, which is getting on for 400 million, barely 1 per cent play cricket. In the villages, where 70 per cent of the people live, the game is virtually not played at all, while in the cities it is played in an organised way only by the better educated classes.
>
> The country constitutes, therefore, an astonishing source of untapped cricketing talent. As natural batsmen and spin bowlers the Indians are as good as any in the world, yet hundreds of millions of them never get the chance to play. Except in Bombay the chances of anyone making the grade from the lower classes are incalculable, and even there they are extremely remote. The point is made only because the popular conception is of a land where cricket is the game of the masses rather than of an intensely exclusive minority.

This is astounding. Mr Woodcock has been touring India for twenty years, yet finds it necessary to explode popular myths now, at the end of a tour which has been massively reported in England. Why? In any case haven't we been told differently? That all Indians love cricket, that cricket will be endlessly popular in India. Three short years ago, after Fletcher's tour of the country, Scyld Berry, *The Observer's* cricket correspondent, predicted in *Cricket Wallah* that India would be the next cricket capital of the world. What has brought about this present change? Why this sudden stress on cricket being the preserve of an exclusive minority?

The superficial reasons are easy to understand. Gower's tour illustrated that cricket, at least Test cricket, was declining. Television, the increasing sophistication of crowds, the poor recent home record of Indians had all played their part. On this tour, apart from Calcutta, Tests have been sparsely attended, non-Test matches hardly at all and, in several places, football has outdrawn cricket. But it is the underlying point illustrated in *The Times* report that is truly significant. Here we have the British view of India, cosily held since the late 1960s, conflicting with Indian reality and leading to doubt and confusion.

The truth is that crowds for Test matches have been declining since the early 1980s. According to some statistics, they reached their peak in the early 1970s, at least in Bombay, which leads Indian cricket both on the field and off. But the early 1970s was the period when the British, particularly Fleet Street, 'discovered' Indian cricket. Though England has been touring India for fifty years, till recently these tours have been regarded as 'B' tours which allowed the major players to opt out of touring for a winter and have a rest. A whole galaxy of cricketers never toured India with England: Peter May, Denis Compton, Trevor Bailey, Godfrey Evans, Alex Bedser, F. S. Trueman, Jim Laker, Ray Illingworth, Brian Close, John Snow, Len Hutton – names that would figure in almost everybody's list of the last thirty years' top cricketers. As late as 1972–3 it was the convention before an Indian tour for the leading cricketers to opt out. The selectors would then appoint a tyro captain – Tony Lewis in 1972–3, Nigel Howard in 1951–2 who had the dubious distinction of only playing for England as Captain in India – to lead a team of a few professionals but mostly young players coming to the top. Thus Tom Graveney and Brian Statham went when they were making their reputations, not as established players. It was only in 1976–7 that for the first time a reigning captain, Jardine apart, took an England cricket team to India.

Not surprisingly the press followed the selectors in treating India as a second-grade touring place. It was only in 1972–3 that a full contingent of the British press went to report India. Before that an Indian tour was reported by stringers, a couple of freelancers and the odd cricket correspondent. It was not until 1976–7 that the BBC began to broadcast ball by ball commentaries. It was in 1981–2 that BBC television arrived, but even today there are no television highlights of the series.

These points are important not so much to reflect the Indian feeling that the British always treat them as inferior – a feeling very prevalent in India – but because it explains how the British have acquired their 'popular conception of a land where cricket is the game of the masses', or a million other misconceptions. It has taken over twelve years for the popular conception to be punctured by facts that have always been known to most Indians.

India is too vast, too confusing for any person to present anything more than a personal view. The Western method which in many ways the Indians have copied, is to try and synthesise India in a manner that makes it sound like a Western country. But you cannot do that with India. There are just too many conflicts and attempts at synthesis lead to despair and resignation. For example, in England middle class means *Daily Telegraph* and Conservative; in India it means a lower-income urban group which reads the Indian equivalent of the *Morning Star* and votes Communist. The Indian well-off definitely do not like to be called 'middle class'.

My book is an attempt to present India and cricket's role in it in its proper historical setting. It is no more than a personal view – the view of one Indian, born in India but educated and moulded by England – a view that both the British and Indians might find unpalatable but which is more valid than the wild romanticism that India and its cricket have been subjected to in the past.

CHAPTER 2

Khel-Khud as Cricket

The day before England met India in the Calcutta Test on their last tour, a small reception was held at the hotel where the two teams were staying. Such receptions are now part of the cricket circus but this one was held to publicise a book by an Indian publisher about the Olympic Games. The irony was lost on the Indians. Cricket is such a potent force in the country that a cricket Test provides an irresistible marketing occasion, particularly a Calcutta Test. The publishers accurately divined that Indian journalists covering the Test would like free booze and food. Cynical as this may seem, much of PR is based on such calculations. I was happy enough to get my copy of the Olympic book – a tribute to the increasing sophistication of Indian publishing – but what took the evening out of the PR rut was a speech of surprising insight by Ashwini Kumar.

Kumar is something of the Brian Clough of Indian sport. Like Clough he is controversial, hated by some, loved by others, though his expertise is hockey, not football. He has had success with Indian hockey, even if his years of stewardship also saw the beginning of its decline, and the successful challenge by other nations to what had become an Indian monopoly. However, his focus that evening was not nostalgic, but philosophic. I had heard a great many Indian administrators talk about sport, but this was something very novel. In a few crisp sentences he demolished the whole idea of Indian sport:

India has no base for sports despite its enormous population. India does not have the wherewithals. Sport in our country is khel-khud (just a bit of fun). It goes against the grain of our country, against our tradition to play sports the way they do in the West. If a child in our country returns from the playground he is not asked by his parents how he fared, but slapped for missing his studies and wasting his time in khel-khud. Sport is against our Indian ethos, our entire cultural tradition. In all modern countries sport is accepted as a part of life. In our country the authorities do not even know what playing facilities are available in our schools. Out of some 600,000 schools we have – and this figure is not verified – some 1.8% have playgrounds. And I am not talking of the vast playgrounds as in the West, but just a little piece of open land behind the school where the children can run, maybe. In a country of 800 million people there are only 11 gymnasiums. The sports budget of the country is 80 million rupees (£5.5m). We are just not organised for sports. The central government does not run it, education anyway is a state government subject so it falls between two stools. There is no dynamic relationship between player and the organisers who run the different sports in this country. Though we are producing coaches they cannot get jobs because the whole thing is not properly organised. In any case the hunger for coaches will not be satisfied till 2059. What we need to do is to encourage school sports between the ages of 8 and 11, something not very expensive to organise.

The views reflected Kumar the military man – he had been head of the prestigious Border Security Force – and probably the anguish of trying and failing to mould Indian sport, particularly the Indian Olympic movement which is a sad story of the bureaucrat trying to make capital of honest, often poor, ill-educated sportsmen. Yet they are quite astonishing. Sporting declines often produce heartrending inquests. Exaggerated pessimism is as much part of the sporting vocabulary as romanticised hyperbole. Just as supporters of winning teams easily convince themselves they are world beaters, so supporters of losing ones readily descend into the slough of utter, inconsolable despondency. But Kumar's analysis is more than that. For it raised the question: 'How on earth did the Indians ever take to cricket?'

It is easy to understand a nation that has no sporting traditions taking to Olympic games like running, swimming, wrestling, even boxing. These have a universality that transcends culture, tradition, organisation. But cricket by its very nature is probably the most organised of games, with a chemistry that is at once subtle and, to the uninitiated, infuriatingly complex. No one who has ever organised a Sunday afternoon cricket match can have illusions about the time and effort required to get twenty-two men, plus helpers together to make it possible. Khel-khud, a bit of fun in some desolate playground, barely adequate to run on, is hardly enough.

So how is it that cricket has prospered in India? Indian Test cricket may be at a low ebb now, having lost a home series to England, but their one-day prowess can hardly be doubted – winners of three impressive one-day tournaments – and capable of producing a host of cricketers led by Sunil Gavaskar who can challenge the best in the world. There is a paradox, though not quite the obvious one which appears at first glance. The paradox is that cricket, the ultimate of team games expressing a philosophy that goes beyond the game, has in India produced neither a philosophy, nor a team, but individuals. It is a measure of the remarkable talent of some of these individuals that India, at various times, has given the appearance of being a team. As the Nawab of Pataudi has said, 'in India cricketers are produced in spite of the system, not because of it'.

Writers on Indian cricket talk of Indians taking to this English game, as the Brazilians took to football, or the Japanese now to golf. Nothing could be further from the truth. India, as a nation, has never taken to cricket. Certain Indians, starting with the princes, for various personal reasons took to cricket. Now more and more follow cricket in India, it is big business and in recent years it has become the sport of the urban Indian. But it remains what it was when the British first took it to India, a game played by certain Indians, often quite accidentally, wretchedly organised, shambolically run which, with the sort of magic difficult to explain, produces cricketers of quality. Pataudi has rightly pointed out that it is absurd to talk of the decline of Indian cricket for this assumes 'there had been a gradual incline'. If his phrasing is odd the meaning is clear. India has never produced a great team, strong in most departments of the game. At certain times there have been good, possibly great batsmen, at others great spinners, lately a fine fast-medium bowler and possibly a great leg-spinner. But the various elements have never fused together. There is no Indian equivalent of Hutton's great sides of the 1950s, or Worrell's West Indians, or Ian Chappell's Australians. India's isolated moments of glory on the cricket field have been the result of one or two towering individuals who have somehow dragged their teams to victory. That is the lesson of Indian history and the story of Indian cricket. And it is only explained by the way that the Indians learnt their cricket from the English.

The story of how Indians took to cricket has often been told. Back in the seventeenth century English sailors wishing to divert themselves played the game in the Gulf of Cambay, it was slowly taken up by the Indians, particularly the Parsis, who considered themselves somewhat separate from the Indians and rather more English than Indians. Indian princes patronised it, Ranji, a minor prince, proved so brilliant that he invented a whole new cricket stroke and inspired legends about him in England. Indians flocked to imitate Ranji and soon this very English game became a national Indian one.

This summary while not inaccurate is like all summaries – a distortion. For it misses out how cricket developed in England between the time the sailors of Cambay introduced it to India and Ranji emerged; or how Indians took to English education and culture. Historians of English cricket have laboured long and hard to trace cricket's origins.

Though the recorded history of English cricket dates from the middle of the eighteenth century, there is some evidence that cricket was played in Tudor times, perhaps earlier. The Black Prince's grandfather played 'Creag' which is said to be an etymological antecedent of the game, and efforts have been made to link cricket with medieval sports such as stool-ball, cat and dog trap-ball and rounders. This cricket was largely illiterate; few records survive and the ones that do are not capable of unchallenged interpretation. While the upper classes had their blood sports – cock fighting and heraldic contests – cricket formed one of the few amusements of the rural poor, part of the amorphous village fair.

Cricket is said to have begun in the forest of the Weald with a curved piece of wood as bat and a sheep-pen hurdle as wicket. This primitive cricket first came into prominence during Queen Anne's reign (1702–14) and began to rival the more popular village football.

Its transformation into the modern, national game that we now know owes much to the public school ethos established by Thomas Arnold and the deeds of William Gilbert Grace. Arnold's Rugby was a mixture of evangelical moralism and romantic idealism seeking to produce Christian gentlemen. Arnold could write a history of the Roman Empire in a tone of such astonishing piety it could all but obscure the violence and disorder that was part of its being – he was trying to counteract the cynicism of Gibbon – and during the opium wars with China he wrung his hands in despair about 'the dreadful guilt we are incurring'.

21

Though sports were not properly organised during Arnold's time at Rugby, by the late nineteenth century the value of team games, particularly cricket as a means of developing character had firmly taken root – and it drew its philosophic sustenance from Arnold's desire to produce an English gentleman who was Christian, manly and enlightened, and one morally superior to any other being.

Arnold's influence was so pervasive that it was soon to be said without exaggeration that 'if a composite history of all the public schools is ever written it will be, in reality, the history of England, since the British Empire has been in the main built up by the founders of the school and the pupils who gained knowledge and had their characters moulded in those institutions'. Sentiments immortalised in Thomas Hughes's celebrated novel based on Arnold's Rugby *Tom Brown's School Days*. In it Tom described cricket to one of the masters as 'an institution'. Arthur, whom Tom has rescued from excessive scholastic work – considered damaging in public schools – says 'it is the birthright of British boys, old and young, as *habeas corpus* and trial by jury are of British men'. The master hardly needs any prompting. 'The discipline and reliance on one another which it teaches are so valuable. It ought to be such an unselfish game. It merges the individual in the eleven; he doesn't play that he may win but that his side may.' We are entering the world of muscular Christianity, the Newbolt man where physical effort and intellectual satisfaction strike a ready equation.

It is interesting to consider why cricket should have been given this honour. Cricket is a subtle game. In form and appearance it can be gentle, even idyllic, yet violence is always there. A fast bowler hurls the ball at 90 mph which could kill a man – and very nearly has – a hard-hitting batsman's use of power is all too apparent to the fielder who is in the path of the ball. The argument between the two can be extremely violent. A fast bowler bowls a bouncer – about the most controversial weapon in cricket – the batsman retaliates by hooking. Yet it is institutionalised anger. Firmly within certain prescribed rules.

In other respects too cricket reflected the nature of British Society. It was – is – a finely structured game. The batsmen are the natural leaders, the bowlers the toiling middle classes, the fielders very much plebeian. Each has its own appointed place, each its own specific task with the game very firmly based on the Augustan principle of order in society.

A basis which was enshrined in the distinction made between gentlemen and players – a distinction considered to be fundamental to the existence of the game. Its removal in the mid-1960s is even today resented by many and said to have led to a decline in quality. The professional was the man who played for money. His competence was unquestioned – he was often conceded to be more skilful than the amateur – but then skill alone has never been the supreme criterion for cricket affection. The amateur represented virtues that were said to have made Britain great. He played not for money but for the love he had for the game, the pleasures he derived, the enjoyment he gave.

It has been suggested, by the revisionist historian Correli Barnett, in his interesting but flawed book *Collapse of British Power* that it was this stress on evangelical idealism and character building, divorcing education from scientific and technological goals, that eventually led to the country's decline. While Germany and Japan gave their educational systems a practical thrust the British produced generations of politicians and statesmen who believed that Britain exercised a 'moral' influence in world affairs and that 'other powers would heed the pursing of British lips and the tuttings of British disapproval'. But perhaps Barnett overstresses the revisionism. If the hard-headed empire-builders, seeking the loot of other countries, were replaced in the late nineteenth century by the high-minded empire-preservers, seeing to prove that the 'British Empire was the best thing that ever happened to mankind' it came from a shrewd realisation that a philosophy was necessary to preserve this curious entity.

Brave hungry adventurers had secured the Empire. Trade had provided the motive and the Empire surplus fed the industrial revolution, but the process had been individual and dramatic. Suddenly, in the middle of the nineteenth century, the British people seemed to discover that they had an Empire. Yet a great many were not sure why this 'tight little, right little island', whose songs and legends celebrated its own exclusiveness, should have suddenly acquired such a huge Empire. While the upper classes were well aware of the benefits of an Empire, a philosophy needed to be evolved why such a huge acquisition had been made and how it benefited the unfed, ill-clothed masses of the urban poor. A history which had always stressed the island's right to remain free of continental involvement now felt the need for a different philosophy, one that would serve an Empire that stretched over four continents. The philosophy that was eventually evolved was service – however spurious – and cricket was to provide a ready symbol.

As with all empires, violence was part of the British Empire. But it was controlled. India was populated by no more than 100,000 British people (a tiny portion of whom bore arms) even though towards the end of British rule the population of the country was very nearly 350 million. To control the Empire the mystique of the sahib was built up: whatever happened all dark skins paled in front of that solitary white one.

Arnold and his heirs may have overstressed the evangelical romanticism but they also realised that gut jingoism, crude nationalism and hatred of foreigners which often affected the urban masses, was not enough to sustain such an Empire. The Empire was a contradiction. The British in their songs and legends conjured up the picture of an island race bravely struggling to keep itself free of continental marauders. *Land of Hope and Glory*'s refrain 'Britons never, never, never shall be slaves' is evocative of this national mood. Yet the Empire enslaved millions of others and this could only be squared by creating the vision of an Empire that was supernational. As Lord Acton would put it in his 1862 *Essay on Nationality*, empires like the British or the Austro-Hungarian ones were the peaks of civilised progress, accommodating inferior races who could be 'raised by living in political union with races intellectually superior'. So the supreme nation-state of our time argued an imperial philosophy that sought to deny other peoples their nationality. It was from such a moral and philosophical contradiction that cricket provided a certain philosophy for the Empire.

The British picture of their island as a beleagured country is, of course, an ancient one dating perhaps from Roman times, a belief strong enough to convert even foreign adventures, like Henry V's conquest of France into ballads of national resistance. Henry rallying his troops before the Battle of Agincourt with those immortal words 'we few, we happy few' could well have been the local commander seeking to repulse a foreign horde – when the reality was quite the reverse. A global Empire, however, imposed different obligations and while the legends of Agincourt were to be recreated in various parts of the world, there was still the need for a philosophy – a philosophy that would try and elevate an Empire founded by adventurers seeking profits and preserved by a strange alliance of merchants seeking to add to those profits and administrators struggling to provide an imperial gloss of service.

'Cricket's influence,' writes Barnett, 'on the upper-middle class British kind with its sense of orthodoxy and respect for the rules and laws and the impartial authority of umpires can hardly be exaggerated'. Barnett's theme may be mocking but the point is well-made. Yet even as the British were fashioning a philosophy for their Empire, their educational policy in India had already begun to produce the first of the Indian leaders who would challenge the Empire.

The Indian educational system was the work of Macaulay. His celebrated *Minute on Education* has been much quoted and misquoted but what has been missed is the debate that preceded it. Macaulay was a liberal of the free trade school with a contempt for Indian education and literature. As he put it in his celebrated Minute, 'I have never found one among them who could deny that a single shelf of a good European library was worth the whole native literature of India and Arabia'.

Macaulay arrived in India to find a furious argument raging between the orientalists who believed that Indians should be taught in their own language and anglicisers who believed that Indians should be taught in English. The debate was framed by the pattern of education in India that prevailed before Macaulay's intervention. It has been best described by Michael Edwardes in *British India*:

> The type of education the British had found when they arrived in India was almost entirely religious, and higher education for Hindus and Muslims was purely literary. Hindu higher education was almost a Brahmin monopoly. Brahmins, the priestly caste, spent their time studying religious texts in a dead language, Sanskrit. There were a number of schools using living languages, but few Brahmins would send their children to such schools, where the main subject taught was the preparation of accounts. Muslim higher education *was* conducted in a living language – Arabic, which was not spoken in India. But there were also schools which taught Persian (the official language of government in India until 1837, when it was finally abandoned) and some secular subjects.
>
> Hindu and Muslim education had much in common. Both

25

used, in the main, a language unknown to ordinary people. Both systems stuck firmly to traditional knowledge.

The East India Company which had steadily, occasionally stealthily, conquered India, had little or no clue about educating Indians – or, for that matter, much desire. They had come to India to trade, had become rulers in furtherance of that trade and wanted to do nothing that would disturb their native subjects and thus harm the profits they were making. They took their cue from the ancient Indian rulers who, except in times of war, left their subjects well alone, content to make money from the land and the commerce. It was only in the Charter Act of 1813 that there was a specific sum allocated to education – all of 100,000 rupees (£10,000) but for many years after that even this piffling sum was not disbursed. As late as 30 April 1845, nearly ninety years after Clive had established the British Empire at Plassey, a total of 17,360 Indians were being taught at government expense in all parts of the British dominions.

These were the result of concessions won by evangelists keen to make Christians of the heathen Indians, and the growing British commercial community in India who saw the value of an English-educated Indian upper and middle classes that could further trade. Macaulay who was both a man of commerce and an evangelist shrewdly combined the two in his celebrated Minute. It was best expressed in his classic speech in the House of Commons on the Charter Act of 1833.

The mere extent of empire is not necessarily an advantage. To many governments it has been cumbersome; to some it has been fatal. It will be allowed by every statesman of our time that the prosperity of a country is made up of the prosperity of those who compose the community, and that it is the most childish ambition to covet dominion which adds to no man's comfort or security . . . It would be, on the most selfish view of the case, far better for us that the people of India were well-governed and independent of us, than ill-governed and subject to us; that they were ruled by their own kins, but wearing our broadcloth, and working with our cutlery, than that they were performing their salaams to English collectors and English magistrates but were too ignorant to value, or too poor to buy English manufactures.

If pure altruism was not the only motive that inspired the British in India, just as significant is the fact that the educational system that Macaulay installed was the classic liberal one. Thus at Calcutta's famous Presidency College, which in years to come was to produce free India's first President and Subhas Bose, who organised an army to fight the British, the education required:

> a critical acquaintance with the works of Bacon, Johnson, Milton and Shakespeare, a knowledge of ancient and modern history, and of the higher branches of mathematical science, some insight into the elements of natural history, and the principles of moral philosophy and political economy, together with considerable facility of composition, and the power of writing in fluent and idiomatic language an impromptu essay on any given subject of history, moral or political economy.

In English public schools the playground was becoming the hot house for the young, in India the same public school-educated administrators concentrated on the classroom. Everything outside it was a void. This has been vividly illustrated in yet another recent book on British India, Philip Mason's *The Men Who Ruled India*. Mason, a former Indian civil servant, in describing the British in India, asks that they should be judged not by their worst actions, or even by their best but by what they aimed at. The introduction eloquently describes how unique amongst nations the English ruling class subjected its young to the bodily rigour of 'cold baths, cricket and the history of Greece and Rome' in order to make them fit to rule India. Yet lyrical as the book can be about the British and their rule there is no description, let alone explanation, of how this bodily rigour translated onto the sporting fields of India.

The index listing for sports – and that includes hog-hunting – is marginally longer than that for servants and there are only three references to cricket. Mason is meticulous in detailing the great and good the British wrought in India. So why ignore cricket? The answer is that the British never actively promoted cricket in India. The English played cricket in India, and the odd administrator encouraged cricket – a Harris or Brabourne in Bombay, Willingdon as Viceroy (though his role was more dubious and political) but there was no master plan to get Indians to play cricket, no educational policy that made cricket part of school life. It was

27

ad hoc, depending on the personal taste of a particular school-master or district official.

It is not that the Indians did not have a sporting tradition. The Indian princes indulged in riding and shooting and soon recognised that one way to curry favour with the English was to organise shoots. The Prince who let the Viceroy bag the biggest tiger when he came to visit, found that this soon translated into useful political returns. Polo was another great favourite with the princes. But this was at an élite level. The sports the princes favoured were the historic ones chosen by ruling classes down the ages – sports as a preparation for war.

Sports as a substitute for war – as in the development of the modern Olympics – was a late nineteenth century concept resulting from the massive changes wrought by industrialisation. England as the first country to be industrialised was to make this idea a central plank of its educational policy. Even today the sporting ethos is probably strongest in this country, and continentals often express amazement about the English obsession with sports. In India the concept never developed.

For Indians, English education was a window on the European world. But a window framed by Indian references. The British changed the language of instruction and the curriculum, instead of religion and accounts, there was a whole host of literary, political and historical subjects – but they did not alter the method of Indian learning.

The classical Indian education in the country's golden age, many centuries before the British arrived, had been wide-eyed and enquiring. By the time the British arrived this had decayed and the Indians who first took to British education – in Bengal they almost demanded it in preference to their own – hoped this would be recreated by the improving alien influence. But while the English education was comprehensive, the methods used to educate Indians destroyed much of its value. Indians may have seen the college-based Oxbridge model as ideal but what developed in India was a mockery of this. Instead of a university or a college where students went not merely to learn from books but from their tutors and peers about life and living, the Indian universities became mere examining bodies. They were like MOT centres of education, checking whether a particular person was good enough to obtain a particular degree. As Judith Walsh, observing the spread of English education in India through the middle and late nineteenth century notes, 'They had no teaching staff and offered no courses. Preparation for their examinations was given by the private schools and colleges that began springing up even in far-flung areas. There was little control over the establishment of these programmes. In fact virtually anybody with the funds to rent space and hire teachers could open a college or preparatory school. A combination of student fees and government grant-in-aid made survival likely and prosperity a distinct possibility.'

The British had two methods of changing this system – to deny grant-in-aid to schools that did not pass their inspections, but more effectively so regulate the examination system so that it provided a uniform system all over the land. Course topics were announced two years in advance and the questions were stultifyingly factual: list the names of the 'twelve Caesars', describe 'some of the chief of our liberties established by the Magna Carta'. Judith Walsh concludes, 'Success demanded a ready memory uncomplicated by imagination or critical judgement. Teachers and students, if they hoped for safety, were well advised to rely on assigned texts, or if they had to choose an alternate, to select one which mirrored the first in organisation and point of view . . . The major, if not the only concern of the student was to pass the requisite examinations'. Their parents had realised the value of English education, they knew a pass meant financial success, failure – ruin. So much so that students who failed even took to putting behind their names 'BA – Failed' just to indicate that they had taken part in English education. The pressure to pass examinations had the unfortunate result that, with few exceptions, the education institutions became glorified crammers where the name of the game was to learn by rote questions likely to be asked in examinations – a tradition that distressingly survives to this day.

This emphasis on cramming helped to create a Hindu work ethic whose tenacity matched the Protestant one. A work ethic that told its children, as the Bengali ditty had it – and still has:

Porasuno kora jey	Those who study hard
Gari gora chorey shey	Get to ride in carriages.

A work ethic based on studies and examinations that is instilled so well that even in his moment of great triumph (three successive Test centuries on his debut), Azharuddin, India's great new Test star, felt obliged to refer to it. Asked what his childhood ambitions were he replied, 'Look, I was never that good in studies to become a doctor or something like that. I always saw myself playing in a Test match; that used to be my childhood fantasy . . . I used to play a lot; studies never really suffered if you know what I mean. I managed promotion each time though as a student I was just about average'. And then the final revealing comment that explains why he is so different from most of his fellow Indians, 'Parental interference was out of question: I used to stay with my grandfather'. Azar, as he is known, ascribes much of his success to his grandfather a devout Muslim who encouraged him to 'pray and play side by side'. All grandparents are indulgent, Indians, perhaps more so, and Azar might have had a very different upbringing if he had lived with his parents. He might have succumbed to the 'good boy' syndrome.

A 'good boy' is defined as one who obeys his parents and diligently memorises his schoolbooks. Not surprisingly the unimaginative nature of Indian examinations gives the mugger an almost natural advantage over the imaginative scholar. Even in this country where Indian students normally do better than their white or black colleagues, their knowledge is like a laser pen-etrating in a single stream – but throwing no wider light outwards.

A stress that made Gandhi, later to be hailed as the Father of the Indian nation, confess in his autobiography, 'As a rule I had a distaste for any reading beyond my school-books. The daily lessons had to be done, because I disliked being taken to task by my teacher as much as I disliked deceiving him. Therefore I would do the lessons, but often without my mind on them. Thus even when the lessons could not be done properly, there was no question of any extra reading.'

Gandhi's school actually made cricket and gymnastics compul-sory no doubt because the headmaster was a Parsee, the first amongst the Indians to take to cricket. But Gandhi 'disliked both' and never 'took part in any exercise, cricket or football, before they were made compulsory'. By the time he came to write his autobiography at the age of 56 he recanted his youthful belief that 'gymnastics had nothing to do with education'. A recantation that echoed that of other prominent Indians – Subhas Bose, for instance, who felt his youthful dislike of sports had probably made him more introverted.

But despite the middle-aged Gandhi's regret he saw no harm in neglecting cricket or gymnastics. 'That was because I had read in books about the benefits of long walks in the open air and, having liked the advice, I had formed a habit of taking walks which has still remained with me. These walks gave me a fairly hardy constitution.' Even for the middle-aged Gandhi, embroiled in a historic struggle with the British, sports was just a means to physical fitness. There was nothing wider or deeper to be gained from it.

Gandhi had ducked, or tried to duck out of gymnastics because he wanted to nurse his father. Certainly parental influence played and plays a big part in the sporting development of the child – more so in India where the family is so predominant. But one reason for the disassociation of sports and general education in India was that by the time it was acquiring its prominence in England a second generation of Indians were being brought up in the English culture who did not share their fathers' values.

Their fathers had hungered for English education, and in the words of one second-generation English-educated Indian, 'our fathers, the first fruits of English education, were very violently pro-British. They could see no flaw in the civilisation or culture of the West. They were charmed by its novelty and strangeness'. The fathers could remember the pre-British days of which their sons had no memory. While the sons and their heirs would unconsciously accept many of the criticisms levied by the English against the Indians, it was the fathers who precisely realised the logic of such English diatribes.

Lack of manliness was a constant British jibe against the Indians and many were the analyses to explain this supposedly unique Indian phenomenon: climate, lax morality, wretched diet and above all, the 'sedentary habits' of the higher classes. There was no dearth of British remedy for this. A. C. Miller in *Seven Letters to an Indian Schoolboy* had warned against excessive scholarship, 'A boy's character is far more important than cleverness at work.' In contrasting Indian and English schoolboys he noted that while not all Indian boys were bad and all English ones good, 'I do go so far to say that English boys as a whole are loyal, just devoted sportsmen'. The Hunter Commission had felt physical exercise 'would have especially good effect upon the minds and bodies of most Indian students. We therefore recommend that physical development be promoted by the encouragement of native games, gymnastics and drill and other exercises of each class of school.'

By the time the second generation of Indians, like Gandhi, were being given an English education, they no longer saw, or at least not with that clarity, what their fathers had seen as a struggle between the ideals of the West and the demands of the old Indian ways of life. Nirad Chaudhuri – probably the greatest writer to come out of the Indo-British encounter – rejected his father's advice to use the gymnastics equipment he had bought for his sons. Regretting this youthful impulse in later life he concluded that he did not have a strong 'constitution' because 'I neglected his advice and in matters of physical culture pursued the bad old traditions.'

Also by this time in the late eighteenth century, just as sports and cricket were becoming the dominant philosophy in English public schools, the second-generation Indians were growing up in a world where Western values were increasingly integrated into their lives. This, as Judith Walsh has observed, meant 'all memory of the foreign origins of these values vanished'. Or if they were remembered it was in a fashion far removed from their origins.

Thus Subhas Bose, who became the great rebel and, during the Second World War, joined the Japanese to fight the British, implicitly accepted the British jibe that Indians were weak and when in London, rebuked his friend for sitting cross-legged. What would the English think of this strange Indian custom? By the time my generation of Indians – the midnight's children of Rushdie's evocative phrase – came to cricket the memories of the English introducing cricket were very dim indeed.

C. L. R. James has described how he took to cricket gulping down *Vanity Fair* with the facts about Grace and Ranji. In the cricket I played in my Bombay school, any link between England and cricket was not so much denied as never alluded to. The two major schools' tournaments in Bombay are the Harris shield for senior boys and the Giles shield for junior boys. Both are inter-school tournaments of great popularity and appeal and I, along with most of my school friends, followed both of them closely. But we had no idea, or even interest in who Harris was, and in any case never quite pronounced Giles's name correctly. We were taught to pronounce it 'Guile' with the 'G' as in Guy and probably thought it had something to do with cows, since *guy* is the Hindi word for cow.

It was many years later, in England, that I learnt about the role

32

played by Lord Harris, Governor of Bombay between 1890 and 1895, in promoting and establishing Indian cricket. I doubt if even a handful of Bombay schoolboys know who the Harris of the coveted Harris shield is, despite the fact that the centre of the shield has a medallion portrait of Lord Harris, surrounded by a laurel wreath. This disassociation between the English creation and the Indian adoption of it, explains a certain Indian contradiction about cricket. The casual English visitor to India, observing the tremendous popularity of Test cricket, may conclude that this means that England, too, is very popular. In fact the exact reverse is true. Those who patronise, administer and provide the money and the fervour for cricket in India today, are perhaps the most fervently anti-English Indians possible. The popularity of cricket is not to be equated with the popularity of England or any values associated with this country. Indian attitude to England is a complex subject, to which I shall refer later, but it is necessary to understand that the Indian love for cricket does not denote a love for England.

True in India cricketing values are accepted, indeed, as many observers have commented, as standards of English cricket have declined, the Indians appear to uphold the age-old traditions of the game. But those Indians would be very surprised to hear that the link between the two is English society.

So if cricket was not rammed down the throats of Indian schoolboys by the English – as clearly it was not – how did it take root? One possible explanation could be nationalism. This certainly explains the rise of Australian cricket. A colony peopled by the British working class saw in cricket a means of getting back at the upper classes of the mother country. As early as 1897 an Australian writer could detect an 'unfilial yearning on the part of young Australia to triumphantly thrash the mother country'.

C. L. R. James has told us how West Indians used cricket to shape their political nation:

West Indians crowding into a Test bring with them the whole history and future hopes of the Island. English people have a conception of themselves wreathed from birth. Drake and mighty Nelson, Shakespeare, Waterloo, the few who did so much for so many, the success of Parliamentary democracy, those and such as does constitute a national tradition ... we of the West Indies have none at all, none that we know of. To such people

33

the three W's, Ram and Val, wrecking English batting, helped to fill the huge gap in their consciousness and their needs.

This happened as the West Indies Federation was struggling to come to political manhood with the different islands agitating for their independence. But no such links developed between cricket and nationalism in pre-British India.

If anything the pre-independence link between nationalism and sports was provided by football. In fact just about the time that Harris, in Bombay, was trying to promote manliness through cricket, another Indian was telling his countrymen:

We speak of many things parrot-like, but never do them; speaking and not doing has become a habit with us. What is the cause of that? Physical weakness. The sort of weak brain that is not able to do anything: we must strengthen it. First of all, all our young men must be strong. Religion will come afterwards. Be strong, my young friends ... you will be nearer to heaven through football than through the study of the Gita ... you will understand the Gita better with your biceps, your muscles a little stronger. You will understand the mighty genius and the mighty strength of Krishna better with a little strong blood in you.

That Indian was Narendranath Datta who would become known to his worshipping admirers as Swami Vivekananda, the first, and probably the most prominent, of the modern Indian gurus. Vivekananda was to successfully preach a form of muscular Hinduism, almost matching Henry Newbolt's muscular Christianity, and a bastard Socialism which was to inspire an entire generation of Indian nationalists and political activists. His theory that India was materially poor but spiritually rich was both an explanation for British rule in India and a balm for nationalist feelings. His belief that India could reclaim her greatness if only she acquired strength would prove so intoxicating to many that it would form the basis for Indian revolutionaries seeking to use Irish-style insurrectionary methods to overthrow the British.

Vivekananda's strength through football ideas were to be brilliantly vindicated on 29 June 1911, when an Indian football team Mohun Bagan club defeated the East Yorkshire regiment in the IFA shield final in Calcutta. To quote the understandable overblown rhetoric of the Mohun Bagan club that day is 'a red letter day in the history of Indian football – a day that has gone down in the history of the nation's struggle for freedom and independence'.

It is worth dwelling on the match. Like all Indian teams, its players played in bare feet. To play on Calcutta's maidan – the vast expanse of green in the centre of the city – was itself an experience. To play in the IFA shield final, the premier soccer tournament in India, against a British team kitted out in full regalia, was more than just a soccer match. Overlooking the maidan was Fort William which, since the days of Robert Clive, had symbolised British military presence in Calcutta and over which flew the Union Jack. Only a few years had passed since Indian football teams had been allowed to play the British and poor Mohun Bagan, with their tiny delicate Indians, gingerly side-stepping the boots of the British, were given no chance against the East Yorkshire regiment. The East Yorkshires led by a goal at half-time, but in the second half, in quite extraordinary circumstances, Mohun Bagan came back to win by two goals to one.

The story goes that as the referee blew the final whistle and the crowd swarmed onto the pitch, one Indian went up to the Captain of the Mohun Bagan team and pointing in the direction of Fort William said 'Brother you have lowered England's soccer colours. When are you going to lower those other colours?' The story may be apocryphal but some of that euphoria is reflected in the Mohun Bagan historian's view of the match that 'it gave hope and pride to all Indians and sustained and strengthened the peoples' feelings of patriotism and helped to rouse a national consciousness. In winning the match and the Shield, the Club had contributed in its own way towards the independent movement.'

Logically, after independence, football should have become India's number one sport. It is cheaper, certainly permeated greater layers of Indian society – even down to the semi-rural areas – than cricket and there were the obvious links between nationalism and football. It is possible that had India won its independence from Britain in different circumstances, cricket might not have occupied the position it does in India today. Had the British been thrown out of India in the violent, revolutionary way, proposed by the Indian nationalist, Subhas Bose, rather than agreed to withdraw peacefully, football rather than cricket would have become the major game. Or had the Bengalis who initiated

35

the freedom struggle, retained their control then football – which is very strong in Bengal – might have become the national game.

But by the time freedom came the national movement was led by Gandhi and his Western Indian allies, with headquarters in Bombay, where cricket had a greater hold. Cricket's path was also smoothed by the fact that Gandhi's campaign was motivated by love, or at least so it appeared. He wanted Indians to hate the actions and results of British policy in India, not the British themselves. Unique amongst nationalist movements, it taught Indians to accept the good that was in the British, while rejecting the harm that they were doing to India and its people. This meant that after independence there was no contradiction in accepting cricket – it could very simply be seen as one of the British goodies which ought to be retained. It was British systems, not the British, the Indians had been fighting, and cricket could be seen as part of the British system of which the Indians approved.

But even this might not have been sufficient but for Nehru's enthusiasm for cricket. While Gandhi was indifferent to cricket (he only once commented on the game and that was to condemn matches between different religious communities in India which he thought encouraged religious sectarianism), Nehru had played cricket at Harrow. Though something of a misfit there (Nehru was at Harrow at the beginning of the century) his love for Harrow deepened as the years went by. Long after he had left Harrow, he became, says his biographer, 'very conscious of his Harrovian connections'. Imprisoned by the British in the 1930s for his politics 'he stuck pictures of Harrow in his prison and drew up lists of poets and politicians who had been to Harrow. He even sensed a certain affinity with Byron on the grounds that they had both been to Harrow and Trinity, and he used to sing the school songs with the younger members of the family ... He was doubtless far happier as an old Harrovian than in his actual years at that school.'

In independent India it was common to see photographs of Nehru, in all white and padded out properly, his head now quite bald but his back fairly straight, playing in the annual Indian Parliamentarians' match. Nehru regularly attended Test Matches and other matches in Delhi, and it was his encouragement that made Delhi a Test match centre. Nehru's biographer provides no clue as to why Nehru should have taken to cricket after he became

Prime Minister of independent India. But just as Nehru felt more Harrovian as he grew older, so, I think, he felt more attracted to English things as he sought to shape an English-free India. Nehru often used to talk about being the first English Prime Minister of India, and probably cricket benefited from that feeling. The departure of the British had removed the moral stumbling block about accepting cricket and this played its part with Nehru, as it did with other Indians.

To my generation of Indians, the first to grow up in independent India, cricket came triply blessed. Blessed by Nehru, who was 'Chacha' Nehru, the universal uncle of all children, blessed by the school and blessed by the community. But it was not presented as a nationalist game, as football might have been. It was not presented as an English game, just a wonderful game which had strong English connections. Though we grew up surrounded by nationalism and with the echoes of the struggle against the British ringing round us, there was no contradiction in promoting and supporting cricket. V. S. Naipaul has suggested that Indians can reconcile historical contradictions only by ignoring historical facts. In others it may lead to neurosis, in Indians it leads to detachment and acceptance. Naipaul is being characteristically severe on Indians, who are not the only ones to ignore historical facts.

The more probable reason is not so much that Indians forgot their history but they, like others – including the English – re-interpreted it. In this version the English subjugation of India was explained in terms of a technological failure. India had nothing to learn from the West in spiritual terms, so the message went – an argument that was re-inforced during the 1960s and 1970s when young Westerners came to India to learn about spiritualism. What had caused the great Indian failure was its inability to keep pace with the technological change in the West. There is some historical justification for this. Akbar, the contemporary of Queen Elizabeth I, undoubtedly had a more splendid court than anything the English monarch commanded – and, in fact, emissaries from Elizabeth were humble supplicants in front of the Mughals. But as the Elizabethan renaissance developed the two countries diverged – India stagnated, England prospered with much help from Indian loot and, if India was to be the equal of the West, she must remedy this technological gap. Of course the theory was flawed since the technical gap had been the result of a moral and educational gap – but Indians could hardly be expected to understand that.

This desire to catch up with the West in technological terms is reflected in every aspect of Indian life. This is vividly illustrated in the reaction to Indian cricketing triumphs. In 1971, for the first time in forty years, India beat England in England, and again in 1983 when, much to everybody's surprise, India won the World cup. Both events were joyously acclaimed and the returning Indian cricketers feted like conquering heroes. The Indian mood was summed up by Mrs Gandhi's reaction to the World cup triumph when she said, 'This shows we can do it'. It was the comment of a technologist who has finally mastered a craft he or she has been searching for. Interestingly Mrs Gandhi's comments were re-echoed some time later in an Indian magazine describing the manufacture of India's first Rover – a welcome break with the rather monotonous old Oxford Morris that clutter the Indian roads. But any suggestion that it marked the emergence of India as a nation would have been quite extraordinary. It would have occurred to no one.

This view of cricket explains why the roots of Indian cricket remain shallow, certainly much shallower than in England, Australia or even the West Indies. Soon after the war Neville Cardus, philosophising about cricket, wrote 'if everything else in this nation of ours was lost but cricket – her constitution and the law of England, of Lord Halsbury – it would be possible to reconstruct from the theory and the practice of cricket, all the eternal Englishness which has gone into the establishment of that Constitution and the Laws aforesaid'. Such a statement would make no sense in India. If everything else in India but cricket were to be destroyed, we would get no sense of the country just from the practice of cricket. We would have some sense of the spectacle of Indian cricket, and some idea of cricket fever that could grip India during Test matches, but nothing more. Cardus may have laid on the aesthetic cream a bit too thickly, but his broader point about the place of English cricket in English society can hardly be doubted. English cricket is woven into the fabric of English society through village, club, county and Test cricket in a very special way. English poets have written about the game, English men of letters like J. B. Priestley have chided their friends who 'have not grasped the simple fact that sport and art are similar activities'. Cricket is the subject of poems and drama and a great deal of literature, much of it contributed by Cardus. There is nothing remotely comparable in India.

No major Indian novelists, or come to that any Indian novelist, has written about the game, Indian cricket does not feature in films except incidentally, nor is it the subject of songs or verses, or anything remotely connected with art. Writers, poets, philosophers reminiscing about cricket in this country could fill many volumes. One such volume *Summer Days*, edited by Michael Meyer, had contributors ranging from Kingsley Amis and A. J. Ayer to Melvyn Bragg, Thomas Keneally and V. S. Naipaul. A comparable list in India would be absolutely impossible. Curiously the only literary book I have seen on Indian sport was written by a Bengali author and was a short story about a football goalkeeper. Now it could be said that this merely reflects the fact that Indian culture is rather more of a verbal one. But even in the West Indian world, where again verbal culture predominates cricket is reflected through calypsos.

Critics could point to the fact that there is a growing Indian literature on cricket. However this is mostly books on cricket written by journalists, or ghosted by them for cricketers. Indian sports magazines do very well out of cricket, and even the general magazines boost their sales during the cricket season by featuring articles on the game. But that does not constitute literature and is rather on a par with film magazines which do very well on the popularity of the Hindi film stars. Indian magazines and books may reflect cricket's status but they do not invalidate the argument that there exists no cricketing literature in India. The game, as it is played now, has failed to develop real, meaningful roots.

The shallowness of Indian cricket can be gleaned from the analysis prepared by Dr Richard Cashman, an Australian historian writing on Indian cricket. Between June 1932, when India made her Test debut, and February 1979, 143 players represented India in 166 official Tests. Of these Cashman has been able to find the birthplace of 128. Fifty-one of them came from Maharashtra, which includes the city of Bombay, eighteen from neighbouring Gujerat and thirteen from Punjab. Eighty-two out of one hundred and twenty-eight came from just three states.

The real, astonishing thing about Indian cricket is not its popularity but the nature of that popularity. It is not cricket so much, but Test cricket that is popular. India made its Test debut even before it had a proper national cricket competition and in modern India, Test cricket has become *tamasha*, a rich Indian word which means fun, excitement and glamour all rolled into one. Just as the Hindi film stars are part of the tamasha – as occasionally are the politicians – so are cricketers. Though Test cricket attracts vast crowds in India and visiting cricketers are mobbed like celebrities and allowed tremendous publicity, the game outside Tests is hardly noted.

Indian newspapers barely manage to report the scores of the Ranji trophy matches, the Indian equivalent of the County Championship. Apart from the finals of the Ranji trophy and a couple of other matches, it is difficult to even get the full score card. The English cricketers, on last winter's tour of India, could have had some appreciation of this had they read any of the Indian papers. I refer to the Bombay *Sunday Observer*, an English-style Sunday paper of 25 November 1984. Its lead story on the sports page is a report of a match between England and the West Zone. The story of the match is fairly comprehensive and includes the photograph of Vengsarkar, the double centurion. Tucked away next to it, with only six lines devoted to it, is a report of a Ranji trophy match between Bengal and Assam. England and West Zone's score card is printed, but there are only brief scores of the Bengal-Assam match. The space given to the Ranji trophy match pales into virtual insignificance compared to a report from Australia on the Test match between West Indies and Australia. Interestingly, the second lead on the page is of a local football match, and is quite well covered.

In India all this is accepted as very much par for the course. It is astonishing to notice the change that comes over an Indian city or town when a Test match is on. In the days preceding a Test, local newspapers are full of news, advertisements and build up of what they call 'Test fever'. Net practices of the Indian and visiting teams take up more space than would county cricket reports in most English newspapers. Photographers are regularly present and almost every act of the two sets of Test cricketers is extensively reported. There are even snippets about the spivs trying to promote a black market in tickets. But as soon as the Test finishes, the fever, like some strange Indian disease, seems to subside. The end of the Test match is taken as the end of cricket and it often vanishes from the newspapers. The newspapers which brought out special editions for Test matches, rarely manage to report domestic cricket scores. Not that ordinary cricket is not popular. It is played by Indians every day on the maidans but in Indian cricket there is no balance between the fervour shown for Test matches and the total antipathy for the domestic game.

The explanation for this Test fever lies not in the deeds of Indian cricketers, but rather the nature of urban India. For Indian cricket is more than a game; it is an essential part of modern industrial India. Ruled by an élite anxious to convince the world that it heads the tenth largest industrial power, one capable of producing atom bombs and exporting food grains and machinery, cricket is an essential status symbol. In the social set up of modern urban India, cricket is one sure way of obtaining acceptance. For the urban poor and lower income groups it forms a valuable distraction from their appalling poverty and struggle to survive. It is important to stress that cricket in India is essentially an urban game, which has yet to penetrate the rural regions which have their own games, very different from the organised family of ball games to which cricket belongs.

It is not very difficult to see why cricket occupies such a position in modern India. The forty years since independence have seen great changes led by a massive, ill-directed, industrial revolution converting villagers into urban dwellers, and producing cities where Manhattan-style skyscrapers co-exist with dismal hovels. The relentless urge to urbanise means that every day hundreds of villagers pour into the cities looking for jobs and security and into Bombay with its film industry come the seekers of fame and fortune. Most of these villagers end up as shoeshine boys, mournfully singing film tunes.

The urbanisation has occasionally threatened to get out of hand. During Mrs Gandhi's emergency rule in 1975–7, the local government in Bombay thought of introducing an entry permit to regulate the flow of such El Dorado-seeking villagers. Bombay is essentially a group of islands connected to the mainland of India and it would be rather easier to control the flow of people into Bombay, than it would be, say, into London. But the very fact that such an idea was proposed reflected both the nature of the problem, and the mind of urban India. Not that such a movement is peculiar to Indians. Cricket became the English national game during the eighteenth century when a predominantly agricultural society transformed itself into an industrial one.

In India, Test matches not only bring together the otherwise strictly segregated classes of urban India, they also make up for the lack of pleasures generally. A five-day Test match with its seemingly endless variations is ideal entertainment and when the cricket gets dull, the crowds can devise their own situations to amuse themselves.

The location of the Test grounds in the centre of modern Indian cities emphasises the tamasha aspect. The cheaper stands are to one side of the ground, generally known as the East Stands. Here on hard concrete, sometimes precariously balanced on planks of wood, thousands gather for their daily excitement, equipped liberally with their own tiffin carriers and makeshift potties, the favourite being empty coconuts.

Movement during play is often impossible. A single gesture can cause whole ranks to sway, and when the play becomes boring the crowd invents its own amusements – occasionally fights. Endless chants which may not be melodious can be effective: B-O-W-L-E-D, as the fast bowlers run up to the wicket; P-L-A-Y-E-D, as a tail-ender, Chandrasekhar, for instance, makes contact with the ball. Fences separate the popular stands from the élite who gather in the colonial-style club houses and elegant marquees. Unlike English grounds, it is almost impossible to walk round the cricket stadium. In any case, such is the crush during Test matches, that it would be hardly worth it.

For those not fortunate enough to get tickets, there is radio or, increasingly, television. On Test days every urban *pan* shop (the Indian equivalent of the corner shop specialising in betel nuts), replaces Hindi film music with All-India radio's atrocious commentary. Work in many offices comes to a standstill, typists, clerks, even the officers, furtively try to catch the latest score. One Indian economist has estimated that five-day Tests cause greater losses in production than absenteeism or sickness!

There are signs that crowds are becoming more discriminating. Administrators have begun to worry about live television coverage during Test matches. In Bombay, India's most sophisticated city, Test fever seems to be abating. India's recent successes in one-day cricket appear to have aroused expectations of continuous success, and during last winter's tour of India it was interesting to note that failure to maintain that success rebounded on the players – and led to loss of popularity for the game. A generation that expected no more than draws is finding it difficult to adjust to sudden wins followed by equally sudden losses. But as

42

long as modern industrial India supports cricket, the game looks secure, providing perhaps the most interesting development since the British left. And it is this cricket Raj that we need to examine if we are to understand Indian cricket.

CHAPTER 3

Middle India and the Cricket Raj

On the afternoon of 1 December 1981, just after 2.30, Bob Willis, the perennial England number 11, plodded forward in his characteristic fashion to a delivery from Kapil Dev. It was the fourth afternoon of the first Test between India and England being played at the Wankahede stadium in Bombay. England left 241 for victory, were 102 for 9. In fact, when Willis had come out to bat, England's position was much worse – 75 for 9 – and Willis and Bob Taylor were involved in a stubborn little stand. But as Willis pushed forward to the second ball of Kapil Dev's thirteenth over, the umpire upheld the Indian's appeal for a catch behind, and almost immediately the emotion and the euphoria that had been building up all day, burst.

For the English it was an unnerving, unreal moment. Keith Fletcher, the losing England cricket Captain, looked beleaguered and hunted. When I interviewed him for the post-match comment, he could barely articulate: 'I have not come here to lose. But there are only sixteen of us against . . .' He didn't have time to complete his sentence as another giant firecracker exploded a few feet away. I was keeping a diary of the tour and I noted some reactions as the firecrackers exploded:

'I know how the Christians felt,' says one awed English man, though I doubt if, even at the height of Nero's rule, there were quite so many firecrackers going off, some even 'from the Pavilion. One disgusted Indian remarks, 'This sort of thing would never happen at the Brabourne stadium (only a mile away and a much more uppercrust Indian place). Too many nouveaux riches and smugglers have become members of the Wankahede stadium.'

At that stage, we rightly concentrated on the cricketing aspects of the defeat, which was to shape the entire series, and put paid to

Fletcher's captaincy. But that little snippet about the clash between the Brabourne and the Wankahede is more illustrative of the cricket Raj which rules India. For it summarises what has been happening in India and the new power barons that control the game in India. Throughout that Test, and a couple of earlier ones I had covered at Wankahede, old Indian friends had bemoaned the loss of decorum and dignity as a result of the move from the Brabourne to the Wankahede. Clubhouse members of the Wankahede had jeered Gavaskar, the winning Indian Captain, when he was made batsman of the 1981 Test match, and even the odd oranges and rubbish had been thrown from the club-house.

It was more than a decline in manners that they were moaning, they were actually railing against the new Indians who had usurped the administration of the game from the old maharajas and upper-class Indians. They were the new Indians, who had benefited most from the undoubted economic progress of independent India, and who were keen to advertise this to themselves and to the world, Indians who were part of what I had called, in a *New Society* article, 'Middle India':

> It is an India that has an embarrassingly high reserve of foreign exchange; it seriously contemplates the export of surplus grain; has discovered off-shore oil; exports machine tools to Czechoslovakia and trekkers to England. It is where Mother Theresa is somebody you read about in the newspapers. It is constantly outraged that the West always spurns its generous overtures.
>
> It would be easy to mock Middle India. It would be possible to doubt it ever exists. Unlike Middle America, it has no distinct geographical area. It is distinct from the familiar stereotypes of opulent Maharajas and diseased Oxfam kids. Basically it represents those who have reaped all the benefits from India's uneven post-independence the ones who have never had it so good and are quite determined to enjoy it, whatever the West might say.

The term middle India may suggest journalistic licence. But the article, from which I have just quoted, was published in December 1977, a few months after Mrs Gandhi had been sensationally rejected in the polls. It was meant to illustrate a certain aspect of Indian élite society neglected, even scorned, by the West. An élite

45

that has been the engineer of the remarkable growth in interest in Test cricket in recent decades in India.

I myself have been part of this middle India ever since my birth. But if hanging concentrates the mind, as Samuel Johnson said, then living abroad brings a totally different perspective on your home country. I returned to India in the mid-1970s after some years living and working in England. Though my ideas were confused, and my life far from happy, the intention was to live in India for good. It was what my parents devoutly wished, and to which I, with a sense of inevitability and acceptance that I find astonishing now, willingly submitted; a working out of the Hindu 'karma'. As it turned out I found it impossible to live in India. The Jesuit rationalism that Father Fritz had inculcated at St Xavier's asserted itself and I eventually returned to this country. But that is another story.

The India I returned to, for what turned out to be a brief sojourn in the mid-1970s, was at a crucial stage. Two months after I returned to the country, Mrs Gandhi's election was set aside by a high court judge in her native town of Allahabad. Indian democrats congratulated themselves on India's democracy – a touchy point in India – Mrs Gandhi, however, saw the judgement as threatening her own private democracy and immediately imposed emergency rule – arresting politicians and censoring the press. India can be a terrifyingly open country, where privacy is hard to find, and not much cared for. Though the bureaucratic maze is horrific – the Mughal bureaucracy built on by the British and run by the most pedantic Hindu civil servants – the system leaves gaps all over the place for individuals to exploit. Thus, for instance, an unlisted telephone number is unheard of in India and home telephone numbers of most politicians, and even senior civil servants, are listed in the telephone directory. Indians love politics and gossip, and freely indulge in both. Mrs Gandhi's emergency, almost overnight, completely changed that. A society which endlessly talked about politics now talked of everything else but politics.

This was brought home to me very sharply a few days after the emergency, in the library of the Calcutta club. This is one of the three great clubs of Calcutta, and it had been impressed on me that I ought to belong to one of them if I wanted to make a success of life in the city. Apart from the library, there was little in the Calcutta club that I found interesting, and it was there that I repaired as often as I could. On that particular June day it was very inviting. The front page lead story in *The Times* was about underground resistance to Mrs Gandhi's emergency rule with the promise of a main article on the subject and an editorial in the inside pages. When I turned to the centre pages, I found nothing: somebody had removed the entire centre section of the paper. I assumed it was the work of some less than dutiful member who wanted to read it in the privacy of his own home rather than the club. As I made my way out of the library, I passed the librarian, and casually mentioned this to him. His reaction was extraordinary. His face became very dark, very heavy, and he said, almost in a whisper, 'Sir, this is a very serious matter. It will be investigated.'

I was somewhat puzzled by his reaction but thought no more of it. I was busily relearning Indian habits and treated the librarian's comments as the sort of over-reaction some Indians are capable of. Soon after I met a relation of mine, who had actually sponsored me for membership of the Calcutta club. He confirmed the librarian's words. The loss of the centre pages of *The Times* had been taken so seriously that the club committee had met. Never, in the long history of the club, had the centre pages of *The Times* gone missing. I don't know what exactly was said at the meeting but something to the effect, I suspect, of the world going to the dogs. If *The Times* was not sacrosanct in the library of the Calcutta club, then what indeed was sacred? The committee decided to seek out the member responsible for this dastardly deed and blackball him. Even now I couldn't take this story seriously and it was the look on my relation's face that convinced me that this was no laughing matter. Eventually, the committee did find out who had committed the foul act. Alas, it turned out to be the censor at Calcutta airport and not a member of the club. Soon after that Mrs Gandhi tightened her emergency rule even further and the censor stopped *The Times* from actually entering the country.

I don't think many middle Indians felt deprived. Mrs Gandhi's emergency rule was very popular in this India. Middle India has always been convinced of its 'work ethic', almost as firmly entrenched as the Protestant kind, and confident that its endless financial calculations will not be damaged by any milk-and-water welfare socialism. Soon after Mrs Gandhi's defeat at the polls in 1977, her successor as Prime Minister, Moraji Desai, firmly rejected parliamentary demands for the dole. Apart from the horrendous financial problems (there are just no estimates of the number of unemployed but they must amount to tens of millions), Desai was convinced that the dole would encourage laziness. In fact most middle Indians, returning from their annual visits to Britain – something they like doing – still express surprise that in Britain you can get money for not working. A not untypical comment is 'People over there are paid for not working. No wonder the country is in a mess.'

Middle India welcomed Mrs Gandhi's emergency, because law and order and firm government are favoured ideas. Mrs Gandhi's emergency rule brought together a package that these Indians had always wanted. No sudden power cuts, which can make life in many cities a living hell, no *bandhs* (strikes) that can immobilise cities for days and no rioting students or workers. Although middle Indians as a class have benefited most from Indian democracy, they are also its greatest critics. It is this paradox that explains the fact that Kemal Ataturk had long been every middle Indian's favourite 'benevolent' dictator. Soon after Mrs Gandhi's emergency arguments were quickly found to support her decrees: a poor peasantry, a huge army of illiterates, a lack of communal sense of discipline.

What was interesting was that even the rigours of emergency did not completely erase Mrs Gandhi's reputation as a liberal compared to the rigidity of her successor Moraji Desai. This was not because of Mrs Gandhi's economic or political policies, but because she touched those aspects of life which middle Indians hold dear. She soft-pedalled prohibition and relaxed foreign travel – things that always meant more to middle India than a free press or an independent judiciary. At the height of the emergency rule I complained to one of Mrs Gandhi's admirers that she had killed free speech. He laughed, 'killed free speech? Why, I have been saying what I like. People who come here can talk freely'. As he did so he waved his arm round his well-manicured lawn, clearly showing the area of free speech that mattered to him. Democractic liberalism, it was felt, excited unbridled populism and Mrs Gandhi's warnings about 'unlicensed freedom' (a very revealing phrase) won universal middle Indian approval. It reflected the genuine fear among many of being sucked back into the growing jungle of mass poverty from which many middle Indians have just emerged.

Not that middle India is a perfectly homogenous group. There is a distinction between those who have fully inherited the mantle of the Raj and those who would like to do so. The former are descendants of the much derided 2 per cent who were anglicised during the Raj and are proudly colonial. Here, almost everybody of some importance knows everybody else. There is a regular flow of political and social gossip, whose intensity and variety over-shadows the established media. This is a society that has taken over all the institutions of the Raj down to the last hallowed club tradition, and even the obligatory Friday buffet lunch. This tra-dition developed during the days of the Raj, when, having written the weekly letter home and deposited it on a 'homebound' steamer, the sahibs repaired to their clubs and had a large, care-free lunch. The weekly letter home and the homebound steamers departed long ago, but the Friday buffet lunch still continues.

It is a world where able imitators of Kipling's Mrs Hauksbee are firmly in charge – and income, status and positions are carefully monitored. Soon after I arrived in Calcutta in the mid-1970s, a Calcutta citizen distinguished the city's three major clubs – Bengal, Calcutta and Saturday – as follows: the Saturday is for young people and those earning about Rs.1,500 (about £150 a month); the Calcutta is for those earning up to Rs.3,000; and the Bengal is for the real 'burra' sahibs and the top executives.

Top executive, in fact, is a favourite middle India phrase. All the classy advertisements and the increasing range of consumer products produced by rapid industrialisation are aimed at capturing his attention. Some years ago when the domestic airlines decided to accept advertisements on products marketed during its flights, it projected itself as a 'powerful new media' to advertisers: 'Top Notch executives, successful businessmen, affluent holiday makers. These constitute a high potential market for all possible goods and services and in India over four million of them commute by air every day. Do you have something to sell them?'

Despite the naked commercialism – and Indian commercialism can be very unsubtle – this has great appeal to the second, more powerful group that makes up middle India. They are part of what is derisively called 'nouveau riche'. Unlike the old established rich, who inherited the Raj mantle, this group's anglicisation is more recent and its grasp of what are considered essential social graces still far from perfect. They are the endless butt of jokes by their colonial élite – jokes that are envious and spiteful. The most despised are the Marwaris – India's fantastically efficient business community. Marwaris originally came from Rajasthan, an arid, poor state in northern India. In Indian legends the Marwaris are pictured as having arrived in the rich cities of Bombay and Calcutta, with just one *lota* (pot) and one *kambal* (blanket) and being so ruthlessly successful in their business methods that while they inherited the riches of the city, the original inhabitants of the city were left with just one lota and one kambal. It is a favourite pastime in Indian élite society to picture pot-bellied Marwaris, their fingers greasy with counting money, emerging from a Mercedes and, then, immediately spitting betel (nut juice) on the roads. It is an image that juxtaposes their wealth and their lack of social manners. The joke goes that if on a hunting trip in the jungle you should encounter a snake and a Marwari, make sure you kill the Marwari first!

Yet it is the money and power of this nouveau riche group that makes middle India increasingly important. Clubwallah, middle India, may resent this but it cannot ignore it. This was well illustrated, some time ago, when I went to interview Shoba Kilachand, then editor of *Stardust*, one of the country's leading film magazines. *Stardust* had made a reputation for itself as being full of racy, film gossip, but Kilachand herself was dismissive of the lives and loves of the Hindi film stars she chronicled. 'I hardly ever see Indian films. I don't know film people, I don't even like them.' She had a shrewd estimate of her public, 'What our readers are interested in is who goes to bed with whom. Many of them are not sophisticated enough to understand what we write. They just cut out our colour blow-ups and worship them, or worse. I don't know. I don't even care.' This was the authentic voice of 'clubwallah', colonial élite India, happy to make money out of the new usurpers, but distancing itself from their tastes.

Perhaps too much should not be made of the differences within middle India. Certain things are common to all middle Indian groups: food, money and power. Indeed they must be the most food conscious group since the disappearance of the Edwardian gentry. Four meals a day – breakfast, lunch, tea and dinner – are obligatory, and these are supplemented by innumerable snacks. Wedding feasts and public festivities are rated by the quantity and quality of food served. For many years there were Government Guest Control Orders limiting both the number that could be invited to weddings and other private functions and the range of food served. Despite this, conspicuous wastage of food is still a mark of social standing. Government newsreels constantly exhort people not to over-eat or waste food.

In recent years the society has become keenly aware of the need for diet control, and American style crash diet programmes are very popular. Middle Indians may not have joined the jogging craze of the West, but they do talk about the need to eat less, and avoid the diseases that flatulence and over-eating bring. In the last year or so there has been lively controversy about slimming programmes and much media discussion about the best way to lose weight. Nevertheless the success or failure of a social evening often depends on the brand of Scotch served, and an inability to distinguish between Chivas Regal and Black Dog can be almost fatal. There are bars in Calcutta where you find a greater range of Scotch whisky than in almost any pub in England. The casual traveller could make a small fortune from reselling a couple of bottles of Royal Salute – a much prized whisky in India. Indians have begun to market their own whisky, under the generic title of 'Indian-made foreign liqueur', but to serve it at a middle Indian party, without adequate backing from Scotch, is to invite social disaster.

This liking for Scotch, inherited from the Raj, is one of the many English factors that bind middle India's extremely diverse communities together. (In Indian terms, English and British are synonymous). Middle Indians call it westernisation which means grafting certain, pleasurable Western ideas onto a basic India, essentially Hindu, framework. Thus the various middle Indian communities follow their own system of separate but equal development: they socialise, celebrate each other's social customs, particularly Christmas, they fraternise at clubs, discos, parties but they rarely inter-marry. Inter-marriage, even between different Hindu communities, let alone between Hindus, Muslims and Christians is rare and something of an adventure.

The most important bond for all the communities in middle India is the need to be educated in English-speaking schools and colleges. When India struggled to attain independence from Britain, abolition of the English language was one of the main planks of the nationalist Congress Party. The Indian constitution decreed that in 1960, English would be replaced by Hindi. But, though Hindi is spoken and understood by most Indians, it remains a northern Indian language, distrusted and derided by most other parts of the country. Attempts to impose it nationwide

51

have been a failure and some years ago, in the great Indian tradition, the constitutional requirement of replacing English with Hindi was neatly sidestepped.

Twenty-six years after its supposed demise, English has never been more popular. The great English-speaking schools, where all subjects are taught in English cannot accommodate all those who want to join. Almost all of them have lengthy waiting lists, starting with nursery classes. Parents register their unborn child at both boys' and girls' schools. Many of these schools are convents or, like St Xavier's, Jesuit controlled. But whatever their structure, the essential and most attractive feature of the schools is the fact that the students there will receive what Indians call an English education. They will learn to speak English from a young age, speak it properly and have some of the celebrated English discipline and values instilled in them. In a recent visit to Bombay, an old schoolmate of mine from St Xavier's, described the harrowing time he had in trying to get his daughter into one of these English schools. The school required that his young girl, about 4 years of age, pass a very rudimentary test before she was admitted. It involved no more than the child showing an ability to talk in English. But unfortunately this child found it impossible in front of strangers, and school after prominent school in Bombay was forced to reject her. Eventually with all hope gone, she suddenly opened her mouth and secured admission. Had she not done so my friend would have found it virtually impossible to find an English-speaking school for his daughter with unimaginable consequences.

Though my friend was far too gentlemanly to actually express it that way, the recital of the story was itself a rebuke of the nouveau riche clamouring to get their children into the English-speaking schools. It is this that has created the rush and produced what is known as the 'daddyji' and 'mummyji' culture. Almost all the nouveau riche children come from a home background where little or no English is spoken. Suddenly at the age of 4 or 5, they are taken to a school environment where everybody speaks English and where much of the education is in the hands of Anglo-Indians. The Anglo-Indians are the physical products of the curious and limited sexual contact between the Indians and the British. During the Raj, the Anglo-Indians enjoyed certain limited privileges at the hands of the British, but found themselves in an awkward position. The British never accepted them as equals – and felt ashamed of these products of inter-racial sex – while the Indians saw them as half-caste interlopers who pretended to be more British than the British. The Indians, interestingly, share the British horror of miscegenation and the Anglo-Indians are still referred to slightingly as *firinghee*'. But as one prominent Anglo-Indian ruefully confessed, this does not stop Indians taking up 'our values – talking English, drinking, dancing – these have become national values, part of the Indian élite'.

The problem for the élite has been to square such foreign, half-caste, Anglo-Indian values with the very traditional Hindu home background. The answer is through 'daddyji' and 'mummy-ji'. At school the children are taught to call their parents, not by the Indian words for father and mother, but by the English terms of daddy and mummy. At home, using a very traditional Indian compromise, the very Hindi word 'ji', which denotes respect, is added to the name. Thus, daddy (English) plus 'ji' (Hindi for respect) = daddyji, a comforting word that seeks to harmonise the English world and the pure Hindu one. One side effect of the daddyji culture is that Indians are now encouraged to intersperse their English with Hindi words. Thus even Indians who have had a convent English education, will use some characteristic Hindi words like *yaar,* which means mate or pal, or *maha* which means great, producing a sentence like 'Are, yaar, that was a maha disco' (Well, mate, that was a great disco).

The old colonial élite suffer this corruption of the English language, something they hold dear, as patiently as they suffer the other corruptions all around them. Corruption, to an extent, has always been part of political and commercial dealings in India and sanctions for corrupt practices can even be found in the Hindu religious text. Nor is India unique in this, for corruption can be found in almost every society. But in India it seems to be omnipresent, an inescapable part of Indian life. Furthermore, while everybody in India is not corrupt, everybody is believed to be corrupt. It was this that drove Mr B. K. Nehru, a cousin of Jawaharlal, a former ambassador in Washington and High Commissioner in London, and Governor of Jammu and Kashmir, to say in a lecture in Madras at the end of 1981 'so immured have we become to it that instead of reacting to it as destructive of all morality and decency, we accept it as a recognised way of life . . . Why have we degenerated in one generation from being an honest society into a dishonest one? Part of the cause is the conversion of a static into a comparatively dynamic society. The changes upset old values but our exposure to wealth is so new that no new values have taken their place'.

Nehru, as befitted a man of his experience, concentrated more on the political corruption and the fact that the Westminster style of parliamentary elections in a country as large as India inevitably leads to a 'direct relationship between money contributed and favour granted'. But, in many ways, his observations abut the change from a static into a comparatively dynamic society and what it has done to values is reflected on the cricket fields and the cricket stadiums of India. There can be little doubt that much of the growth of Indian cricket mania, the millions of rupees that have led to the rise of new stadiums, have been fuelled by 'black money'. This is money accumulated by Indians in all walks of life at the expense of the tax payer. Money which fuels a parallel economy where every transaction has two parts: a white part and a black part. The white part is the one you declare in official contracts and reveal to the tax man. The black part is the real genuine one, not written down, not accounted for but without which the transaction would not take place. Thus in Bombay, where flat prices are higher than in London, you would have to pay 60 per cent of the price of your flat in 'black' money and only 40 per cent in 'white', tax-accounted money.

There can be little doubt that some of this black money, or 'number two account', as the Indians call it, has gone into cricket and contributed to Test cricket fever in India. There are no statistics available, but the simultaneous growth of Test cricket fever and number two accounts seems more than mere co-incidence. Almost anybody in Bombay will tell you that a good many of the season ticket holders, whose prepayment funded the Wankahede stadium did so through their number two accounts. This may be the malicious gossip of those who lost out to the nouveau riche, but nobody who has monitored the progress of Bombay in the last two decades can doubt the existence of black money.

During the decade 1970–80 there has been much change in Bombay: new buildings, land reclamation. Perhaps a symbol of this change has been the extension built to its most famous hotel, the Taj Mahal. This is, probably, one of the greatest hotels in the world. Nobody who has experienced its service, or its luxury, can easily forget it. The hotel, itself, is ideally located – overlooking the

Arabian Sea and right opposite the gateway of India, the very spot where George V arrived in India in 1911 to hold his famous *durbar*. Yet the old Taj Mahal had an oddity that one could never quite explain. You would expect the front of the hotel to face the Gateway of India and the arch that commemorates George V's arrival. Yet what looked like the back of the hotel faced this while the front, with its tree-lined gravel driveway was approached through a rather dingy, mean street at the back.

There was an explanation for this, and this was that the Taj Mahal hotel had been built by the rich Parsee industrialists, the Tatas. Some time before the Tatas decided to build the Taj Mahal, one of them sought entry to an English club in Bombay. In the days of the Raj, English clubs were strictly segregated, and did not allow any Indians, except as menials, and the rich Parsee was refused. In fact he was further insulted to find that there was a sign outside the club saying 'Indians and dogs not allowed'. His response was to build a hotel, the Taj Mahal hotel, and put up a sign outside saying 'British and cats not allowed'. Of course, this is an apocryphal story and is meant to indicate the clever way in which Indians responded to British racial arrogance. But as the story was told to us it had a sad end. The rich Parsee industrialist hired a European architect to design the hotel and send the plans out to India. But when the plans were received in Bombay, they were either received wrongly, or interpreted wrongly and the hotel was built back to front. The architect is supposed to have committed suicide, though this could not prevent the oddity of the Taj's entrance facing away from the sea.

The Tatas have always denied the story but almost everybody in Bombay believes it. More significantly, and this underlines what I was saying about change in Bombay, several years later the owners of the Taj Mahal hotel decided to do something about the entrance. Next to it there had been a small, but rather well-regarded hotel, called Green's. This was one of those classic, colonial hotels in Bombay, very popular during Christmas and New Year's Eve and much valued for its cuisine and its Anglo-Indian and Goan dance bands. The Tatas acquired Green's, decided to expand their hotel and this time there was no question of where the entrance was. The old entrance at the back remains – and rooms in the old wing of the hotel are still very prized, but the new entrance, one that is regarded as the main entrance now, has a modern driveway which leads straight from the Arabian Sea and the Gateway of India into the Taj. To me this change has always seemed to symbolise what has happened to Bombay in the last decade or so. If you like it is the difference between cricket at the Brabourne stadium and cricket at the Wankahede stadium.

For almost four decades from 1937, cricket in Bombay, and very nearly cricket in India, was represented by the Brabourne stadium. It was named after Lord Brabourne, the British Governor of Bombay at that time, and to most people in Bombay it was known as CCI, short for the Cricket Club of India. In Indian eyes it was the Lord's of India with CCI having the status almost equal of the MCC in this country. To gain entrance to the pavilion of the Brabourne stadium you had to be a member of the CCI, and that was never easy. There was always a long queue and membership cost thousands of rupees. Not only was it a magnificently constructed stadium, but the pavilion cum clubhouse had luxurious rooms where players could stay and, if they so wished, watch play in their dressing gowns. Apart from normal club facilities – lounge, card and ladies' rooms, and cocktail bar – the end of the day's play would see the ground itself converted into an open air dancing hall with a wooden floor erected on the outfield, near the clubhouse. The major difference from Lord's was that while the pavilion at Lord's would not admit ladies, except the Queen, the CCI quite encouraged society ladies to be guests. On important match days they could be seen seated, in their glittering saris, in the Governor's pavilion next to the clubhouse.

But if CCI was cricket to most of us, its relations with the rest of Indian cricket were never very smooth. The official cricket body in Bombay was the Bombay Cricket Association, which actively resented the haughty colonial style of the CCI management. The main problem was the allocation of Test match tickets. A whole block of seats, over 17,000 were given to the Bombay Cricket Association for distribution to its various clubs, gymkhanas and associates. But the BCA never considered this adequate and every Test saw a familiar battle develop between the CCI and the BCA about the allocation of tickets. There were strong personalities involved: Vijay Merchant, on behalf of the CCI, and Mr S. K. Wankahede, on behalf of the BCA. If Mr Merchant had his cricket pedigree, he had been one of the country's finest batsmen and a well-known broadcaster, Mr Wankahede was prominent in politics, including a spell as the Finance Minister of the State of Maharastra. Perhaps the row was inevitable. Mr Wankahede and the Bombay Cricket Association were flexing their administrative muscles in the way the Maharastrian cricketers of Shivaji Park had done almost a decade before while Merchant is a Gujerati, from one of the old money families of Bombay. But it would be wrong to see the fight that developed between the CCI and BCA, and led to the development of a separate stadium, as a purely Maharastrian versus non-Maharastrian fight.

It was more of the old money versus new money argument. Certainly nobody could doubt the existence of the new money as Mr Wankahede and the Bombay Cricket Association made its response. Almost as soon as the last Test of the India versus England 1972–3 series was finished in Bombay, the BCA made it known that it was to be the last Test to be played at the CCI. It was as if the Test and County Cricket Board had declared war on Lord's. Bombay had heard many such arguments before, though never so emphatically, and it did not believe Test cricket would vanish from the 'dear old CCI'.

Even as the West Indies arrived in India in the autumn of 1974, it seemed most unlikely that a Test match at Bombay could be staged anywhere but at the CCI. Mr Wankahede had promised a new stadium, even selected the place, but the stadium was far from constructed and it was difficult to see how, within a few short months, it could materialise. However, when the West Indies returned to the city in early 1975 to play the final Test of the cliff-hanging series, they found that the Wankahede stadium had, in fact, come into being, with the result that Bombay has two first-class stadia within a mile of each other.

It was one of the swiftest constructions in Bombay history. It seemed to demonstrate the power of money in Bombay. As Dilip Sardesai had said, contrasting Bombay with Madras, 'in Madras money was solid', while in Bombay 'money flows' – in this case from businessmen who had learned to manipulate Nehru's Fabian socialism to make their own fortune.

The clash between old and new money is not confined to India, or cricket, nor all that recent. My father was exposed to such arguments almost thirty years ago. A business acquaintance invited him to dinner in his palatial home in Malabar Hill. The house looked rather decrepit from the outside, but was oppulently furnished inside. The contrast seemed remarkable but during the dinner, the business acquaintance explained to my father 'You see Bose Sahib, we are not like these new business people who have come to Bombay and made a lot of money. We are *baniadi* rich (the old landed rich), we don't have to display our riches like these new people'. It was this that explained the difference between the decrepitness of the exterior and the lushness of the interior. My father later learnt that actually the business acquaintance was very much part of the new rich. He had made his money recently, then bought the decrepit house but was so keen to be seen as part of the old, landed gentry rich, that he had left the outside decrepit, while furnishing the inside lavishly.

The new rich of Bombay no longer feel it necessary to present themselves as part of the hereditary, landed rich. They may, or may not, be proud of the ways in which they acquired their money. The Hindu system imposes few sanctions and the post-independence growth has removed the colonial cum ritualistic Hindu reticence which made my father's acquaintance so keen to be part of the *ancien régime.* Now they are keen to explore avenues which would display their newly acquired wealth. Even a casual visitor to the main Indian cities can see the new rich in the bars and restaurants in the mushrooming five-star hotels, swanking down mean, rutted streets in Mercedes – much prized as a status symbol in middle India – and at important social and art functions. But it is cricket, this very English game with its very English nuances, which provides the ideal theatre. In that sense cricket could be said to have been created for middle India. Just as Pascal felt that if there wasn't a God we would have to create one, middle Indians might well say that if there hadn't been cricket, they would have had to invent it. Some of them, sometimes, give the impression that they have indeed invented it.

It is easy to see why cricket should appeal to this group of Indians. Cricket, probably more than any other game, is, essentially, an intensely ritualistic game. The charm lies in the fact that within strictly defined parameters and rituals, it provides scope for infinite variation. Suspense builds up during the length of play, as for instance in the memorable Headingley Test of 1981 between England and Australia. It is difficult to imagine such a turn around in another game. Soccer is played for ninety minutes and does not quite allow for the slow build-up of tension as does cricket. Headingley illustrated this perfectly well; until lunch on the final day most realists had to go for an Australian victory, only to find England dramatically turning the tables in the afternoon.

Cricket and its rhythms have just the right feel for middle Indians. As one Delhi journal, observing the crowds gathering at Ferozeshah Kotla said, cricket was 'just another of the props for a successful day-long picnic'. It was during the first Test in Delhi, in the 1972–3 series between India and England, that the Indian newspaper *Statesman* captured the way middle Indians could take to a Test match.

The Modis are rich industrialists based around Delhi. For the Test match they had established their own 250 square yard barricaded enclosure right in front of the pavilion, surrounded with four fairly large signs of 'luminous green and red', that proclaimed it as the 'Modi Enclosure'. Throughout the day's play the enclosure was a hive of activity, but it was at lunch that it acquired its real significance:

A low table approximately 4 yards × 12 yards was laden with food. Behind it stood two drumfuls of drinking water. A liveried servant, impressive in his all blue, gave the signal and the guests, including evidently the scions of the DDCA (Delhi and District Cricket Association) patron family, left their chairs nearby to be served . . . A former Cabinet Secretary and a former Inspector-General of police were among the frontliners in the enclosure. There was any number of other officials, including a former Union Deputy Minister and a Rajya Sabha (Indian House of Lords) member.

It is cricket as *tamasha*, that rich Indian word which conveys fun, excitement, glamour and suspense, all rolled into one. It was tamasha which made Test cricketers rival film stars and Mrs Gandhi, when she was alive, in popularity. There are some good economic reasons for tamasha. Just as the Hindu film industry mixes glamour with money, so does Test cricket in India, particularly for the businessmen who support it so lavishly. Tests bring together the rich, the not so rich and the aspiring rich in one convenient setting. The Indian lower income groups tend to describe themselves as middle class, a term which does not have the same meaning in India as it has in England. In India the word middle class can be used by the low income clerk who fervently supports the communist party to the fairly well-positioned executive, whose views are somewhere to the right of Genghis Khan and his income almost ten times that of the clerk. Both executive and clerk probably work for the industrialist who sponsors cricket. Outside the office their lives would rarely meet, except in a stadium where a Test match is being played. This is what makes Test cricket in India such a unique cultural, even political, occasion.

But this is not all – Test cricket also provides a golden commercial opportunity. Gathered, in one convenient place, are most of the people who have purchasing power in the Indian urban economy. Sponsoring cricket means reaching this crucial public immediately. This explains the nature of commercial sponsorship in Indian cricket and the existence of a plethora of awards. So many that when Chris Tavaré was made man of the match in the Third Test in Delhi during the 1981–2 series, for his century, he found himself with not a solitary award, as in England, but with nearly half a dozen: a television set, a thermos flask, an attache case and, even, a scooter. Wisely, Tavare had already arranged to exchange his awards for Indian rupees, rather than lug them all back.

The commercial sponsorship of cricket and the money it has attracted from middle India has undoubtedly been good for Indian cricketers. As I arrived in Bombay in November 1981, to report the India versus England Test series, it seemed that nearly all the English cricketers had been recruited by Indian advertising agencies to promote some or other Indian product. Boycott, amidst cover driving, was advising Indians either to drink Seven Seas cod liver oil or fly Cathay Pacific jets, the adverts taking up almost a quarter of the dreadful sports pages of most Indian papers. Botham had linked up with Gavaskar to promote tea, and nearly every Indian newspaper or magazine seemed to have the syndicated thoughts of Botham, Fletcher and many others. There was some talk in Bombay of the English players being a bit too greedy but I could only admire their self-restraint. The game seemed to be used by almost every consumer company in town to sell its products. On the drive from the airport to the city, past some of the biggest and most wretched slums in India, there were numerous advertising awnings using cricket to sell their products. One local butter manufacturer showed its mascot struggling to tie the laces of his cricket boots underneath the slogan reading: 'If you dilley-dalley, butter will melt', a reference to the boot problems that Graham Dilley had on this tour. All this made me feel that the cricketer visiting India could well take the position adopted by Clive when he was accused of making too much money in Bengal in the eighteenth century, he replied: 'given the riches that were offered to me, my Lords, I am surprised at my own modesty'.

Some of the industrialist patrons of middle India frankly acknowledge the reason for their cricket patronage. One of the more recent ones is Virenchee Sagar, managing director of the Bombay firm Nirlon which employs Sunil Gavaskar, and has made a determined attempt to establish itself as one of the leading commercial cricket teams in Bombay. Sagar makes no bones about the fact that since success in cricket brings the company free publicity and goodwill, cricket costs should be seen as a reallocation of the annual advertising budget. Promoting a product or a company may not be the only objective and many of the middle Indian industrialists talk of using cricket to develop a more professional and businesslike approach in their own company. Discipline is something highly valued in India – but rarely found. Urban India, as Professor Galbraith said, can be a functioning anarchy. It was this that made Sanjay Gandhi's talk of discipline and slogans of 'talk less, work more' quite so popular with so many middle Indians. India's besetting problem, they believe, is 'indiscipline' and the discipline and concentration required to succeed in cricket is much valued.

Promoting cricket as tamasha can have side affects. Just as everybody wants to see a successful show, so everybody in urban, middle India wants to go to the Test match. This may be changing because of the spread of television. But perhaps the most evident effect of Test cricket as tamasha is to be seen in the long hours local journalists spend just before a Test match, arranging and deciding who gets the tickets. The reason is that there are so many applicants that the cricket authorities have decided that press tickets are best handled by local journalists' associations who can detect the genuine from the less serious. Every little hick journalist, it seems, wants a ticket even if it be the annual *Tandoori Recipe Cookbook*. In Bombay for the first Test in the 1981–2 series, the local journalists' association had to whittle down requests for tickets from 135 journals to a more manageable 85. As one local journalist put it 'some times we get requests from street publications and how could we put its editor next to John Woodcock? What a shame it would be for India'. Even then for that Test match I sat next to a press man, who was in fact the marketing manager of his newspaper, clearly not reporting the cricket but for whom getting a Test ticket was one of the perks of his job. It indicated social standing in the community.

Perhaps the best way to capture the flavour of cricket as tamasha is to visit Calcutta during a Test match. I did that for *The Sunday Times* during England's tour in the winter of 1984–5. This is how I reported the preparation for the Calcutta test:

For the past week the Calcutta police have been guarding the home of a middle-aged Indian businessman. Though his house is only a few hundred yards away from the homes of the British diplomatic community, the police are protecting him not from possible enemies, but from 'friends' wanting tickets for the Third Test match, against England starting tomorrow. For 43-year-old Jagmohan Dalmiya, secretary of the Cricket Association of Bengal and Mr Fix-it of the match, all of this is part of the phenomenon that is a Calcutta Test. A phenomenon that produces an estimated 85,000 crowd for each of the five days of the match (Dalmiya claims a more precise 78,811) with possibly a few thousand outside clamouring to get in.

Despite poor crowds so far on this tour, Dalmiya, like an impresario sure of his product, has never had doubts. 'There has been a decline even in Calcutta' he admits, 'but my requirement has always been 300% of capacity, so "house full" is no problem'. He's in a good position to judge. Within hours of the end of the Delhi Test, his telephone had started ringing: 'Normally I don't get calls till after eight in the morning. Now it starts ringing at half-past six, and mostly from people who have just remembered that they are my friends.'

Some of the interest is due to England's surprising win at Delhi to level the series, but even before that locals were convinced that Eden Gardens would not fail to come up with that special magic of India the younger England players had been told about, but have yet to experience. Indians call it 'Testmatch fever' and that is perhaps not an inappropriate phrase. For very like a real fever, it has been building up, almost visibly, on the streets and round the England team's hotel.

Almost every activity of the England players, including the Christmas Day fancy-dress party, was extensively reported. As the England team left their Calcutta hotel for last Thursday's one-day international in Cuttack, a crowd of several hundred suddenly gathered in the way they do in this city.

For many in Calcutta, that is the closest they will come to seeing the cricketers. For others with a little more money, the last two weeks have been a search for a 'ticket'. In Calcutta, you don't have to explain what the ticket is for. Businessmen have had tax inspectors drop hints that a ticket or two would help with assessments, bank managers have suggested a similar leniency towards borrowers and to accommodate the demand for press tickets Dalmiya has had to divide journalists between 'working' and 'non-working'.

Perhaps nowhere can you experience Calcutta's special Test fever better than in the tent opposite the cricket ground that is the home of the Calcutta sports journalists' club.

Normally it is like any other journalists' club, perhaps a bit shabbier, with writers trading stories that are part of journalism's charm and cynicism. But in the past week it has taken on the look of an Indian railway station as leading Indian cricket journalists have queued to get their 'tickets'. In most Test centres, press tickets are distributed by the people who run the match. In Calcutta, the authorities have happily abdicated this responsibility to the journalists simply to avoid charges of favouritism.

So last week the most wanted men in Calcutta, after Dalmiya, were the executive committee members of the journalists' club, whose job it has been to whittle down the 1,000-odd applicants to 250. As Kishore Bhimani, sports editor of the local *Statesman*, puts it 'We get applications from all sorts of people. One year we even had people claiming to represent Paris Match and Der Spiegel. In the weeks immediately before a Test, we suddenly have sports magazines being published that nobody has heard of, and they disappear almost as soon as the Test is over.'

One reason for this great hassle is that in Calcutta you can't just go to a ticket counter and buy a ticket. No daily tickets are sold, or even 'season', meaning five-day tickets, as elsewhere in India. The only source open to the general public is a curious lottery where some 900,000 lottery tickets are sold, out of which emerge 8,500 lucky Test-ticket holders. Otherwise you have to 'know somebody', or belong to the right organisation.

Dalmiya argues that this very odd system evolved in order to deal with the problems created when day tickets *were* sold.

In 1969 a stampede, as thousands queued for tickets, led to seven deaths. In those dark days it was common for Calcutta cricket administrators to issue more tickets than there were seats, and such characters often went 'underground' to escape the wrath of the public.

The mechanics of distribution are only part of the explanation for ticket fever. The rest lies in the curious nature of the city. It is predominantly a centre of Bengalis, but where the money is in the hands of the acquisitive and fantastically successful Marwari business community.

The Bengalis despise the Marwaris as carpet-baggers, and hold them responsible for the post-independence decline which has seen Calcutta fall from being the first city of the East to one that most Indians try to avoid. Plagued by power-cuts of several hours a day and incessant political strife, Bengalis find there is little to celebrate except their very typical Bengali 'hujuks'.

The word means roughly 'intoxicated enthusiasm' and in the past Calcutta's 'hujuks' have included riotous welcomes for such disparate characters as Krushchev and Pele. In India Test cricket is an occasion for the various sections of urban society to come together in a fiesta. But as television eats into this audience, Calcutta retains its enthusiasm for the real thing.

To return to the question of patronage, Dr Richard Cashman, in *Patrons, Prayers and the Crowd*, has analysed the role of contemporary patrons, highlighting their changing nature, and the impact of the *Times of India* inter-office tournament. As he says, this must be one of the most unique tournaments in the world with nearly 300 office teams entered in seven divisions. What is interesting about the analysis is the light it throws on the old money versus new money development of middle India. Early winners of the *Times of India* tournament were old established organisations: utilities and government concerns, such as the Bombay Electric Supply and Tramways Company, BEST for short. In fact BEST was the most successful of pre-independence *Times of India* teams winning the shield six times in eight years between 1937 and 1944. It was one of the first to realise the need to recruit good cricketers and of the need to give cricketers time off for daily net practice. Indian independence marked the heyday of the BEST cricket team – though it did win the shield again in 1952 – but as post-independence industrialisation progressed, the old utility companies, the railways and the customs teams fell away to be replaced by commercial firms.

Interestingly, the initial successes in the new phase of the *Times of India* tournaments were achieved by Tatas, very much a firm from the old money Indian tradition. The Tatas had been led by a succession of Tata family members interested in sport. They began to make their mark with the foundation of the Tatas sports club in 1937 and won the *Times of India* shield for the first time in 1941. In the days of my own boyhood maidan cricket in Bombay of the 1950s and early 1960s, much of the cricket in the city was characterised by what we saw as the epic clashes between Tatas and another Indian company called Associated Cement Corporation, ACC for short. The Tatas-ACC matches in the *Times of India* shield used to rival Ranji trophy matches at the Brabourne stadium and at times attracted a bigger crowd.

ACC had started life as a British company, though it was slowly, successfully, being Indianised. In the 1950s, with rapid industrialisation and urbanisation, making cement and cement products became all the more important ACC expanded quickly. So did its cricket team as it successfully recruited some of the top Test cricketers: Desai, Sardesai, Wadekar and Inrajitsingh. Yet despite this talent, ACC often lost to Tatas, largely because of the performances of Bapu Nadkarni, the mean Indian left-arm spinner. In a sensational move, which was the Bombay equivalent of the English-style soccer transfers, ACC successfully poached Nadkarni from the Tatas by offering him a better job. The poaching came just after Nadkarni's feats had led to ACC's defeat in a fascinating *Times of India* shield final. The excitement generated by this transfer was not matched until another cricketer was poached, this time from the ACC – and almost twenty years later. That cricketer was Sunil Gavaskar and the poaching was done by a very new firm, reflecting very new money, Nirlon.

Virenchee Sagar, Nirlon's managing director, is in many ways the archetypal new middle Indian. Though not much of a cricketer, he is a keen student of the game, close to it and a contributor to many Indian cricket and sporting magazines. Sagar is dismissive of the old patrons of Indian cricket, like the princes, and his company's stated aim was to build up a good team recruiting Bombay state players on the threshold of their careers. While Sagar has generally held to that policy, in 1978 he made a significant decision in recruiting Gavaskar and this established Nirlon as the most important team in Bombay. Led by Gavaskar, it now has a near Test side which includes Ravi Shastri, widely tipped as India's future captain and the great heart-throb of Indian cricket, Sandip Patil and the former opening bowler Ghavri. Nirlon, specialising in synthetic textiles, is part of the new industrial scene of India and interestingly its cricketing rise challenged the dominance of Mafatlal, which in some ways represented the somewhat older industries. Mafatlal started in textiles but has diversified into chemicals, garments and even plywood. Its prominence in the *Times of India* tournament almost exactly mirrored its economic expansion. It first won the shield in 1969–70 and then almost established a stranglehold, winning it continuously between 1971–2 and 1977–8. The company recruited shrewdly and widely, among them Contractor, now the wise statesman of Indian cricket, Ashok Mankad, son of the great Vinoo, Eknath Solkar and rising stars from other Ranji trophy teams. By the end of the 1970s Mafatlal was the team of Bombay, glittering with stars that very nearly made up the Test side. However, in 1984, splits within Mafatlal decimated the company and the cricket team. Mafatlal, largely a company owned by the family, split up as a result of dissension between the Mafatlal brothers. The effect on the cricket team was immediate and catastrophic – it broke up and has virtually disbanded. This leaves Sagar's Nirlon team the undisputed champion of Bombay cricket and is likely to remain so until another commercial sponsor comes along.

For a time in the mid-1960s and 1970s it seemed as if commercial sponsorship would face a challenge from state institutions – particularly the State Bank of India. The State Bank represents neither new nor old money but the power of the bureaucracy, and provides an aspect of middle Indian involvement in cricket which should be considered. The State Bank of India is a nationalised bank – the largest bank in the country. After Mrs Gandhi nationalised the major banks of India in 1971, the State Bank began to acquire an important role as pivotal bank in the economy. Mrs Gandhi had nationalised the banks principally in order to persuade the banks to lend more to the impoverished rural economy and so encourage enterprise there.

The results were very different. Nationalisation led to the growth of banking in India but a growth more in the urban and semi-urban areas than in the rural ones. The banks themselves and their managers became very powerful and connections were formed between Indian industrialists keen to secure loans and bank managers, the managers being keen to provide for their retirement, perhaps by a seat on the board of a public company.

The State Bank of India's heavy promotion of cricket in the mid-1960s and early 1970s was dramatic. Not only did it win the *Times of India* shield four years running between 1966–7 and 1968–9, but at one stage the State Bank of India team could probably have fielded an eleven that could do battle with almost any Indian eleven. Players included: Bedi in Delhi, Vishwanath and Kirmani in Bangalore, the elegant left-hander Ambar Roy in Calcutta and the mercurial Milkha Singh in Madras.

But between 1970 and 1976 cricket recruitment virtually ground to a halt as it was decided that sportsmen should receive no special favours in terms of recruitment and that they should enter the bank through the regular competitive channels. During the 1970–6 period the State Bank did not recruit a single player and the one first-class cricketer who entered the bank did so on his own academic merits. It was feared that Indian cricket would suffer if the State Bank did not resume its patronage. However, this has not occurred. New sponsors have come up, and keep coming up. As industrialisation progresses, and new industries spring up, they need an outlet for their products and cricket provides an ideal medium.

Perhaps the oddest thing about the growth of middle Indian cricket is the civil service connection. Without the help, indeed the blessing, of the civil servants, cricket in India could never have expanded in the way it has. In India, as elsewhere, cricket is built round tours. India entertains overseas teams like England, Australia and the West Indies, and, in turn, tours abroad. In India such touring arrangements require government sanctions, not for political reasons, but for pure economics. Since the early 1960s India has suffered from a severe foreign exchange crisis – so severe that at one time Indians travelling abroad received just £3 in foreign exchange – that was certainly the amount I was allowed to take out of the country when I left it for the first time in 1969.

Yet this was also the time when the pattern of reciprocal tours between India and the major Test-playing countries was established. In those days the weeks preceding a Test tour of India always provided a familiar scenario. The Indian Cricket Board would announce the tentative dates of the tour and then murmur, almost *sotto voce* that it couldn't guarantee the tour because it would have to secure permission from the Indian Finance Ministry for a release of exchange. The Board officials would hurry to Delhi to hold discussions there. There would be leaks and whispers in the newspapers, and eventually, as the public veered between despair and euphoria, the news would come that the tour had been saved and the Finance Ministry had released the exchange. Of course, this may have been the ministry officials playing their part in an enjoyable cricket drama, but it has always seemed extraordinary to me that Indian Test cricket began to blossom in the 1960s at a time when the country was cutting back on many things. This, at a time, when India's performances on the cricket field were by no means golden. India had returned from the 1959 tour of England having lost all five Tests. Again in 1962 India returned from the West Indies having lost all five Tests. However, Finance Ministry officials, persuaded by the Indian Cricket Board, provided cogent reasons why the hard-pressed Indian Exchequer should release scarce foreign exchange to finance disastrous cricket tours.

An example of the power of the civil service was revealed when in November 1981 attempts were made to block the England tour because the English team contained Geoff Boycott and Geoff Cook who had played in South Africa. After a great deal of drama the tour was approved. When I got to Delhi I was curious to know how the controversy had started. My friends in Delhi suggested that it was all the work of certain dissatisfied senior civil servants. It seems that during the previous Delhi Test, these civil servants did not get as many tickets as they wanted. This considerably angered them and they decided to teach the Indian Cricket Board a lesson. It made some nice publicity for India in the right Afro-Asian circles and, in the end, established Mrs Gandhi, who finally allowed the tour, as a benign, considerate statesman. All the while the Indian Cricket Board was sweating and wondering what would happen. No lesson could be more dramatic. Apocryphal the story may be, it is quite plausible and an illustration of the power of Indian bureaucracy. Without the support of this bureaucracy Indian cricket could never have prospered. In many ways the bureaucrats were like the new middle Indians using cricket to advertise their power. Just as India's post-independence growth had given money to the middle Indians, so India's Soviet-style planned economy had provided the civil servants with the power to influence events. Modern Indian cricket derives its strength from the money of the industrialist allied to the power of the civil servant. Yet for the old money industrialists of Bombay this alliance must seem superfluous.

Perhaps the most emphatic illustration of the old money attitude to Indian cricket is provided by Vijay Merchant and his family firm of Thackersey of Bombay. This is one of the old established mill-owning families of Bombay, part of the Gujerati textile owners who shaped the city. Merchant's name is actually a misnomer, because he should be Vijay Thackersey. But when he was trying to explain his name to his English principal, he took so long and got so involved in the intricacies of the Gujerati family, that the principal decided that, since Vijay clearly belonged to the merchant class, he would have the surname Merchant. Vijay was to make his reputation as a cricketer under that name and, now, happily confesses that 'I am the only Merchant in the Thackersey family'. Merchant's contribution to Indian cricket is immense. He was, arguably, the first Indian Test cricketer to display the professionalism and dedication normally associated with English cricket. Since his retirement Merchant has been active as a commentator, and a fund raiser for various charities. Yet, despite the wealth and his position, the Thackerseys have never had a prominent cricket team in Bombay. They are far too well established, far too well known, to require cricket to establish their name. Vijay Merchant, one suspects, must feel an odd sense of satisfaction that he established his cricket name not under his ancient family name, rich and secure as it is, but a borrowed name given by an impatient English man. It is unthinkable that any middle Indian would have accepted that.

CHAPTER 4

The Gully, the Maidan and the Mali

When I started writing this book, the kindly man who edited it suggested to me that I explain how a 7 or 8 year old in India takes to cricket. We know how he does so in this country but surely the Indian process is very different? Indeed it is. If English cricket is essentially rural and village cricket, in George Orwell's picturesque phrase of the light falling towards evening and a ball hit for four killing a rabbit on the boundary, Indian cricket is urban. Its roots lie in the lanes of India's teaming cities and on the broad patches of green, called the maidans, that occasionally break up the monotony of concrete. Talk to almost any Indian Test cricketer, particularly of the last thirty years, and he will trace his cricketing roots back to the maidan and the gully. The wonder of the maidan is well captured by Budhi Kunderan, in this recollection of how he started playing cricket:

> Since my parents moved to Bombay, when I was eight years old, I hadn't seen cricket in my native place. None of my family members (have) ever seen or played cricket in their lives. The first time that I saw a cricket match on a maidan in Bombay I fell in love with the game . . . this is the only game we could play on the maidan, apart from running, to play any other game in Bombay (in) those days you had to be a member of big clubs, where you could play tennis or other indoor games. But I had no opportunity as such.

An evocative picture of Kunderan, the villager moving to the big city and being claimed by cricket, sufficiently early for India to have a remarkable wicket keeper and batsman. Similarly, gully cricket, often with a tennis ball, was part and parcel of the make-up of almost every Indian cricketer – as much part of Viswanath's batting, as Chandrasekhar's bowling, or even Azharuddin's rise to fame. It was gully cricket at the old MLA ground of Hyderabad that

70

started Azharuddin off and he and his mates getting together and forming a gully team provided him with his first taste of cricket.

All this can be simply stated. But how does one convey gully cricket? It does not have the natural cadences or the rhapsodic melody that comes naturally to English cricket. It can be hard, brutish, often messy, though with a beauty of its own. It would be tempting to draw shrewd analogies between cricket in England and gully cricket in India, as has been attempted with beach cricket in the West Indies. But I can best convey it by reminiscing about the gully cricket that I played at Bombay's Flora Fountain – the very heart of this great city.

The centres of the world's major cities are well etched in the mind: New York's Times Square, Paris's Champs Elysée, London's Piccadilly Circus. But even now I feel a curious magic about Bombay's Flora Fountain. We called it the heart of the city and so it was. The Flora the fountain commemorated was lost to history, even the various ladies who made up the fountain could barely be discerned and only occasionally did their mouths and nostrils and breasts spout water. As a child I could remember Flora Fountain trams but as the city removed trams, the fountain took on its more recognisable Indian shape of a haven for urchins, layabouts and stray dogs amidst a large parking lot. Round about it swirled Bombay's commercial traffic.

We used to say with pride, and occasionally from my mother, a little disgust, that all roads led to Flora Fountain. My mother's disgust was due to the fact that our house acted as a magnet for all sorts of visitors, most of them uninvited. To me, from my bedroom window, it seemed to provide a panoramic view on the world: here the cinema, there the bank, here the school, there the playing field, here the sea, there the restaurants. Much has changed in Bombay in recent years as Manhattan-style tower blocks have gone up and the city has fallen prey to property developers. The rhythm of Flora Fountain hasn't changed.

Flora Fountain at seven in the morning is expectant: the sound of a passing bus distinctive. By nine it is a cacophony of noise, as cars, buses, taxis, handcarts, lorries and horse-carriages make their way towards the various business houses round the area. By twelve the hubub is pierced by the rhythmical chants of the 'box-wallahs' balancing tin boxes on their heads and carrying hot lunches for the hungry clerks. This must be the most remarkable

71

food service in the world, with almost each individual office worker in Bombay receiving and eating the lunch faithfully prepared by his wife at home. By three the constant afternoon noise is again pierced – this time by a different cry, that of the news vendors selling the evening papers; 'Evening, Evening, Bhumi'. By six the noise has hardly abated but now the centre is a maze of queues as commuters patiently wait for their buses. By nine the streets are virtually deserted, or as deserted as they ever get in India, and such is the contrast in noise that a fast moving taxi braking hard can produce a jolt. It is twelve before silence really falls and then the streets surrounding Flora Fountain are a sea of human bodies: the homeless of Bombay making their beds on the pavements. It was a rhythm I had grown up with, yet it so fascinated me that even on holidays I would often sit at one of my bedroom windows and observe the pattern, so regular and yet so capable of wonder.

Our flat was on the second floor of an office block almost exactly opposite the Flora Fountain. The block itself was one of a chain of linked houses which stretched across what the American would call a 'block', and for reasons that I never fathomed out, all the houses in the block had names associated with the sea. Our house was called Sailor Building but I had never seen any sailors in it, the house next to it and linked with it was called Darya Building, which literally means 'the house of the sea'. Down below was Bombay, with its swirl of traffic, its hawkers and its almost endlessly fascinating variety of shops. Just past the American dry food shop and the picture gallery, which appeared a bit too highbrow and snooty for us, ran a lane where my father's company had its main Godown, and just to the right of this lane, past the cold drinks shop, the betel nut place and the area's most elegant tailor, was my friend Hubert's magical cricket gully. From my flat to his gully was no more than two hundred, perhaps three hundred, yards – a walk of less than a minute, yet our worlds could not have been more different. It was our amazing St Xavier's School which brought us together but it was cricket, and gully cricket, that cemented our friendship.

There was nothing sweet about Hubert's gully. The entrance to his gully was narrow, as if it were a pencilled afterthought of the architect designing the area. On one side there was a high wall that enclosed the Parsi *Agiari* – the Parsee religious place, a formidable barrier. The other wall opened with the area's sewer and

72

ended with Hubert's house. The sewer part of it was open, while underneath Hubert's house was situated a press which reeked of gum and paste and sticky molten substances, a shop of sorts and then a gymnasium where in the evenings the local boys – poor but enterprising – could be seen developing their puny bodies.

The structure of Hubert's gully was of some importance. Its narrow entrance meant that cars – or in fact any form of transport – was never particularly welcome – the high wall of the Agiari and the definable boundary of the open sewer on the other gave the area the appearance of an enclosed space. It provided a sort of mini-cricket field all to ourselves, where Hubert and I, mimicking cricketers we had admired, could play out our fantasies. Even here our relationship was defined: I, the Bengali Hindu, assuming the names of Indian Test cricketers, while Hubert, the western Indian Catholic, invariably assuming the names of English or Australian cricketers. Years later he was to tell me that he had gone to watch his first cricket match – the 1956 Australian Test match at Bombay – in expectation that one of the Australians would go down with stomach trouble and Hubert, from the cheap-priced East Stand, would be drafted in to fill the breach. To me the fantasy in the story was Hubert being asked to play Test cricket at all. It did not seem strange to me that Hubert, whose skin colour and appearance were not all that dissimilar to mine and millions of other Indians, should expect to play for Australia – with a name like Hubert Miranda that seemed very natural.

Neither Hubert nor I had ever been properly coached in cricket. At weekends or holidays we watched proper cricket on Bombay's maidans, I had read a few instructional books, seen a bit of Test cricket and generally discussed the game with my friends. Now Hubert's gully fashioned all this into a very strange game. I emphasise, it appears strange now but then it seemed most natural, even the stench of the sewer which was always strong in our nostrils. Our pitch was the road – stone chips and coal tar; three lines drawn on the wall that divided the gully from the rest of the world were our wickets. The road was sufficiently long to simulate a full-length cricket pitch and, conveniently at the point where the bowler's crease would be located, there was a manhole with a cover. It seemed ideal to mark the spot of the bowler's wicket. Beyond that there was another few yards where the bowler could indulge in a run-up and, if necessary, this could

73

be increased by running parallel to the wickets, alongside the gymnasium, a run that was not only quite long, but rather elegant since it provided a curve as you approached the wicket.

The hazards of the gully seemed to increase our appetite for play. Though we had drawn the wickets on the wall as straight as we could, the wall markings as wickets meant that there was always an element of doubt as to whether the wicket had actually been hit or not, doubts that were not always easy to resolve since the bowler's interest invariably clashed with the batsman's. To this was added the hazard of the sewer. The very nature of the gully, a wall at one end, shops at the other, meant that we could only bat at one end. This meant that the sewer was our permanent square-leg and a firmly hit ball, or even a rustic swing, down the leg-side, often landed right in the middle of the sewer. Not that we were squeamish about going in to collect our ball. We, generally Hubert, would balance on the wall and precariously fish out our rubber ball. However, this did cramp our leg-side shots and our general tendency was to play on the off-side.

Both Hubert and I had played our early cricket with a hard ball and were petrified of being hit on the legs. So our normal tendency was to retreat from the ball down the leg-side and poke it away on the off-side. In Hubert's gully this was also a very paying stroke. A mere five yards from the wicket was the wall of the Parsee Agiari and to stab it in front of us and towards cover, our most favoured stroke, ensured it would hit the wall. The convention Hubert and I had devised meant that any hit on the wall of the Agiari was worth two runs. We occasionally managed to drive straight ahead hit the doors of the gymnasium or the printing press and this counted as four, a mighty hit landing on the first floor verandahs outside Hubert's house counted as six. Very occasionally our swings cleared Hubert's house, which was roughly mid-on, and dis-appeared somewhere into south Bombay.

Every now and again it cleared the high wall of the Agiari. The Agiari was cover, to sewer's square leg, but here the problem, if anything, was much worse. From the sewer you could retrieve the ball, the Parsee Agiari was a total loss. To approach the Agiari with its closed wall and forbidding atmosphere demanded a courage which neither Hubert nor I possessed. We had occasionally tried it and had been mortified by being confronted with Parsee gentle-men, skull cap on their heads, and wearing the all-white Parsee garb of vest and loose trousers, standing sternly at the entrance, almost defying us to try and retake our ball. In histories of Indian cricket, much is made, and rightly, about the role played by Parsees in fostering it. We knew little about this history, our knowledge of English cricket history was substantially more than that of the Indian one and for us, Parsees, at least the Parsees of the Agiari, were not initiating our cricket but destroying it.

There was one other source of interruption. I have said the seclusion of Hubert's gully made it ideal. But it could not be entirely protected from what went on in the wide streets surrounding it, and every now and again the interaction of the Bombay police with the Bombay hawker stopped our games. Hubert's gully, as I have said, was a mere two hundred yards from my home, and the main road through south Bombay which ran right up to Victoria Terminus, the gothic Victorian building which was Bombay's main railway station. All along the pavement, from our block of buildings right up to Victoria Terminus, a whole group of hawkers sold their goods to the public. Their place of business was the pavement, their method of selling highly fascinating and their whole operation quite illegal.

The problem was that the hawker was not left unmolested. He had to contend with the police, not so much the man on the beat, who probably received a regular sum of money from the hawker called *hafta* which allowed the hawker to carry on his pavement business. It was the sudden police raid, in a very black police van, which caused the hawker and our cricket, problems. Sometimes the local policemen would tip the hawkers off and they would take precautions but occasionaly the raids came as a surprise. No sooner did they see the police van approach, than the hawkers quickly gathered up their things. Hubert's gully, a quick run away from the police, but secluded enough from the rest of the world, was a very convenient hiding place. Suddenly in the midst of the most tense India-England Test match, with me as Umrigar trying to avenge myself on Hubert Trueman, we would find that we had suddenly acquired an extra wicket keeper, or a couple of slips, or even a hawker-fielder at silly mid-on. It would become impossible to continue playing. Occasionally the panting hawkers, running for shelter into the gully, would be chased by the police fanning out from the van. Armed with *lathis*, they would rain blows on these unfortunate hawkers and frog-march them, whimpering and complaining, to the police van. I must confess that such was our dedication to Test cricket, that we shed few tears about this.

We were definitely on the side of the police dealing with 'hawker nuisance', a favourite Bombay phrase, as this meant we could carry on with our cricket.

Of course when all else failed, when it rained, or it grew dark, or Hubert's gully was somehow occupied, there was always the landing outside my flat. It was no ordinary landing, reflecting the fact that the house was never meant to be lived in but just used for offices. Our flat had really been carved out of a large office floor, the main and best part of it – facing the road – was our flat and the one at the back, my father's office and store room. The result was that when you arrived on the landing outside the flat, any number of doors faced you. The first one as you came up the flight of stairs was a door that led to a row of toilets. Next to it was a much larger door which led to my father's office and storeroom. Next to it was another door which was always shut, a third led to our kitchen and then finally there was the main door. This started off by being a rickety, rotten door, smeared with heavy chalk marks which denoted wickets. It slowly developed into a better-looking, more permanent door, against which we placed a specially constructed set of wooden stumps fixed to a base.

Its advantages were obvious. It was enclosed and gave the feel of an indoor wicket, we could easily play at night as the landing was fairly well lit. It was, however, much narrower than Hubert's gully and did not give us the same feel of a cricket pitch. The landing itself formed the wicket at the point where the staircase from the floor below curved on to our floor, marking an imaginary bowler's wicket. But this severely restricted our run-up which had to be of a curving, slanting type to have any meaning whatsoever. The only way we could increase our run-up was to open the door that led to the row of 'loos' immediately behind the bowler's wicket. Running along the length of this and emerging from darkness, one could gather some speed and simulate the feel of what we imagined was a quick bowler.

As in Hubert's gully, cover was again a problem. In Hubert's gully it was the forbidding wall of the Agiari. Here, cover point was a window. At some stage early in our India-England-Australia Test matches, a window had been broken and never replaced and a sizzling cover drive, or what passed for it, meant the rubber ball whizzing through the open window and dropping two floors below right down the common sewer of the three buildings. To collect this ball was an extremely difficult feat and invariably I had to seek the assistance of some of my father's servants, or, more usually, have it replaced.

But perhaps the gravest problem with my landing was that it was, after all, a landing of a flat and, therefore narrow. A leg-side stroke was almost impossible since the wall on the leg-side was a few inches away from where we took guard at the wicket. And then there were the problems of the two staircases – the one that came up from the floor below and the one that went to the floor above. Very often a straight drive that beat the bowler would ricochet off the wall and go bouncing down the wooden stairs – right down to the flat of an old lady, who would complain piteously.

It is possible Hubert and I fashioned a unique form of cricket but I doubt if our experiences were all that different from many of the midnight children growing up in India in the 1950s and 1960s. If anything our experiences of cricket were typical of India then, and now.

From gully to maidan was a natural transition. In fact we journeyed back and forwards between the two forms of cricket very often, as do almost all those who play cricket in India. The maidan is, probably, the most evocative place in Indian urban life. It has been called the equivalent of an English park but this is grossly misleading. The only similarity it has with a park is that it is a vast, open area, very often at the centre of cities. But beyond that there are no similarities. It is not merely that the grass in an English park is much greener and finer than that of the maidan, but that whereas an English park is an oasis of calm, a shelter from the hustle and bustle of city life, the maidan reproduces Indian city life with all its noise and clamour. The grass is matted, raggy, struggling to stay alive amidst the dirt and rubble. Flowing through the maidan are little canals, the surface is pock-marked with ditches, even what looks like small ravines and the whole area is filled with people from every walk of life. It is amidst such confusion and noise that Indians learn to play their cricket.

The photographs in this chapter, taken at the Fort William maidan in Calcutta, on the rest day of the Calcutta test, illustrate what maidans and maidan cricket are like. There is the maidan cricketer who fancies himself as Dr W. G. Grace, a pavilion under the tree, tea with cakes from a tin box, the bewildering variety of cricketing styles and dress and above all the sheer wonder of playing cricket on a ground so inhospitable you might think it would deter walking, let alone the pursuit of such a delicate game.

But just as the lotus, that great Hindu flower, springs from the dirtiest and most inhospitable of surroundings, so does Indian cricket arise, grow and blossom on these maidans dotted all over the urban landscape.

Nowhere can maidan cricket be better appreciated than Bombay, particularly south Bombay, where I grew up. That area is dominated by three great maidans: Azad, Cross and the Oval. Azad, meaning free, had the distinction of being the home of the club to which Vijay Merchant, one of India's great batsmen, belonged. Opposite is the Cross, so called because at one end of it there is a huge cross bearing the inscribed legend INRI. Azad is a regular venue for many of the matches played in the inter-schools tournaments of the city. Cross often attracts large crowds to watch famous Tests, or ex-Test players playing in the inter-office *Times* shield tournament. This competition, organised by the leading local daily, *The Times of India*, is very well reported and, at times, an even better draw than the Ranji trophy. It costs nothing to watch and it is not unusual for a few thousand people to gather along the boundary edges, sometimes spilling over onto the adjoining roads, to watch the stars of today and yesteryear do fierce competitive battle. This is what may be called *mali*-dominated cricket.

Malis generally live in the shacks that dot the edge of a maidan and efficiently police the pitches on the maidans. These pitches are distinguished from the rest of the field not merely in the normal cricket sense, but by special arrangements. No sooner is a cricket match over than the mali comes trundling in with wooden staves and ropes and encloses the whole area of the pitch. It would not take much to remove the wooden staves and dismantle the ropes but such is the aura possessed by these illiterate, but shrewd guardians of the pitches of the maidan, that nobody dares. Also playing on these pitches is part of a package that you have to earn. Along with pitch comes a tent, specially erected for the match, and acting as a pavilion and changing rooms. A tent that comes with a little cubicle attached to it and serving as a lavatory. It is when the malis start erecting the tents that the people on the maidan know that a proper cricket match, on a proper pitch is about to be played.

The maidan pitches are also used for net practice – mostly on weekday afternoons. The Azad maidan lay between school and home, and on my way back from school I would occasionally pause to watch these cricket nets and find nothing surprising in the fact that the batsmen, with their boxes happily attached outside their trousers, practised at the nets. Today when I revisit Bombay, and occasionally visit Azad maidan, the sight of hundreds of batsmen in full cricket regalia proudly displaying their boxes as they practise the forward defensive stroke seems odd, even faintly obscene. Then it was part of normal mali-maidan-cricket.

Most of my maidan cricket and, for that matter, most people's, was played on dirt tracks with some grass on it which formed the space between the pitches. This wasn't the only impromptu part of our cricket. There was the problem of equipment. I had been generously provided with full cricket gear, some of it from my father, and some of it gifts from friends and relations. But most of the members of my team were not quite so happily placed, and in most of our matches we had at best two pairs of pads, and very often just three pads. I mean not three *pairs* of pads, but one pair of pads and another solitary pad! So for much of the time, since most of us were right handed, we wore a pad on the left leg, leaving the right unprotected. Gloves were a scarcity and, though I had a set of stumps, only very rarely did we play in matches where we had two sets of stumps. Generally we had four stumps which imposed its own constraint. Three stumps would constitute the wicket at one end, the solitary stump the bowler's wicket at the other end. This meant that at the end of overs the batsman would cross over, not the wicket keeper or the fielders. Again the bat which had been a gift of a friend of my father was our prize bat, and very often the non-striker would have to do with a broken bat, or a wooden plank. At the end of an over, or when it was his turn to bat, he would exchange his bat, or plank, for a proper one. These are, of course, personal recollections but they mirror cricket as it was played then and now.

Not surprisingly maidan cricket gave rise to a new vocabulary. Thus maidan cricket uses the expression 'runner' in a totally different way from the common cricketing meaning of the term. In cricket a runner is one who runs for a batsman who has been injured during the game and cannot run for himself. In maidan cricket the number one batsman is called the 'opener', his partner is called the 'runner'. Very often in this class of cricket there are only three stumps and the stumps at the bowler's end are indicated by a pile of *chappals* – Indian slippers – heaped at the spot where the proper stumps would be. The runner is the one who immediately takes up his position at the chappal end.

There is also 'twoodie'. In maidan cricket boundaries have to be laboriously fixed. There is often very serious arguments about where the boundaries of the ground are. This is not surprising since the ground is not marked out, there are very many matches taking place all at the same time and the square-leg of one match is the cover point of another match. Often there are objects on a maidan which conveniently indicate a boundary: a roller, a tree, perhaps the spot where a pitch has been protected by the mali's wooden staves and ropes. But very often there are insurmountable objects on the ground too near the wicket to classify as a four and a hit to the object is denoted as twoodie, meaning two runs.

But perhaps the most major innovation of maidan cricket is the reinterpretation of the two fingered salute. Now, normally in cricket the index finger of the right hand raised upward into the heavens is seen as the traditional mark of the umpire's decision in favour of the fielding side. This is all very well when the umpire is giving a decision in favour of the fielding side. But what if he is signifying not out? How does he do it? He could say 'Not out', but in maidan cricket this is considered not enough. So an innovation has been introduced whereby one finger raised to the heavens is out and two fingers raised to the heavens is not out. In maidan cricket, the umpire wishing to turn down an appeal doesn't say 'not out' or shake his head – a gesture which in India has a very different meaning – but raises two fingers of his right hand.

But what sort of cricket is this maidan game? Let me reminisce again and talk of the maidan cricket I played as I grew up in the 1950s. For some reason, and may be because I provided much of the essential gear – stumps, bat, gloves, pad – I was the Captain of my maidan team. In the early years I also provided two very important players: Shankar and Arjun. Shankar was my father's driver and Arjun one of the many servants which my father employed. Both of them were young men in their prime and though they hadn't really played cricket properly, their ability to clout the ball hard and bowl it faster than we could added considerably to the strength of our team. This enabled us to boldly challenge older boys and hold quite an advantage over most teams. Later, as work commitments made Shankar and Arjun unavailable, I formed a team that perhaps reflected that area of Bombay rather well.

Apart from Hubert, whose cricket skill was perhaps slightly inferior to mine, there was Bala. He was some years senior to us

80

and of his origins, we knew nothing. One day while we were practising at the Oval he had turned up and become part of our team. He would often come in bare feet, or at best wearing thin, fragile chappals. I think his father was some sort of labourer and his family lived in a *chawl*, a tenement not far from Flora Fountain though, prudently, we made no enquiries.

Then there was Eddy. He was the same age as Bala but came from the same Catholic mileu as Hubert, though from Goa and, of course, was much more sophisticated and cleverer than Bala. Both Eddy and Bala, I believe, appeared for the matriculation at the same time, with Eddy doing somewhat better than Bala. This gave Eddy and Bala a certain awe in our eyes. In school, matriculation was always being held up as the great exam that would crown our school career, passing it was considered essential if our lives were to have any meaning, and we hoped to follow the example set by Eddy and Bala.

I was personally intrigued and enchanted by Eddy's infatuation with *The Guns of Navarone*. This was around 1958 and *The Guns of Navarone* had just been released in Bombay. It was proving immensely popular and easily notched up a Silver Jubilee, twenty-five weeks of continuous showing. Eddy, if I remember rightly, saw it half a dozen times and appeared to have memorised every scene. His particular favourite was the moment when David Niven and Gregory Peck discover that Peck's girl friend is really a German spy. Eddy, in a typical Goan accent, that would now be described as a take-off of Peter Sellers's Indian one, would love declaiming David Niven's speech to Gregory Peck urging him to kill his girl friend. 'Do it for England', Niven urged Peck in the movie and this became Eddy's war cry during our matches. Eddy, who was quite a decent bat, would often share stands with me and in the middle of a stand, as we crossed over, or consulted in the middle of the pitch, Eddy would seek to encourage me by quoting Niven's speech and saying, 'Do it for England.' I don't know how often we 'did it for England' in those matches but we found nothing incongruous in Eddy's exhortation.

But perhaps our most colourful cricketer was Ching, the Chinaman. It was an indication of our cricket, or at least of my team, that we never really discovered his proper name, nor even made any effort to do so. He lived not far from the dock areas of Bombay and had been introduced to the team by Bala. The most distinctive thing about him was not his origin, which we accepted without question, but his style of play. His most effective, in fact his only, stroke would be to cross his legs in front of the wicket and then hold his bat in the gap formed by the crossing of the legs. If he kept the bat straight then he would drop the ball dead centre. Occasionally he would twist the bat either on the leg-side, squirting the ball through fine leg, or on the off-side, sending it through slips. I think the shock of the style proved so great for most bowlers that they often found no way of dislodging Ching.

Bala, Hubert, Eddy, Ching and I would form the hard core of the team. We would be supplemented by other players, cousins of Eddy's or friends of Bala's but at times we struggled to complete the team. Then total strangers would be incorporated into the side. Some of them just people lounging at the Oval while we were about to start the match. This gave our already exotic team an even more exotic flavour and probably accounted for our success.

Some of our most colourful matches were played against a team made up from the residents of Rehmat Manzil, a large block of flats on Veer Nariman Road, the road which ran past the Oval and houses most of Bombay's restaurants. Many of the boys in the team were from my own school, some of them from my own class, and they were the archetypal 'building' team (all being from one building). There was Gupta, who happily allowed everybody to mispronounce him as 'Gupte' thus appropriating some of the glory that was attached to the name of Subhas Gupte, India's legendary leg-spinner and a hero of our youth. The cricketing similarity between Gupta and Gupte was remote, since Gupta's leg-breaks very often turned out to be gentle up and down stuff. Worse still not all members of Gupta's team accepted his captaincy, though the gravest problems for him were caused not by his middle-class school contemporaries, but by Sammath, the son of the 'building' durwan, an Indian-style porter. Durwans in India generally hail from Afghanistan or the North West Frontier provinces and are called Pathans. Most of them are called not by their names but by a general term, Lala, and this Lala was a tall, fierce man who fitted every Indian stereotype of the Pathan and looked capable of fulfilling his job of protecting the building. Sammath, his son, in our cricket terms was just as fierce – a tearaway fast bowler who took a long run up and appeared to deliver the ball with exceptional speed. Unfortunately for Gupta's team, Sammath also had the fast bowler's temperament and did not like being taken off at any time. This caused some merry rows between Sammath and his Captain Gupta, much to our joy.

No doubt individual memories of maidan cricket will differ. But in essence I doubt if it has changed all that much. It is still the world of twoodies, runner, the V-sign signifying not out, the mali as a shambolic man but with real power protecting his pitch from the assaults of the multitudes and the maidan team made up of many elements reflecting urban Indian life.

CHAPTER 5

Ranji's Burden

So far we have discussed the puzzle of Indian cricket. A country that is cricket-mad turns out to be not so much mad about the game as mad about the spectacle that is associated – or it has created – around the game. A game that is played in the country not in the structured, organised fashion of village to club, club to county or state and then to national team as in England or Australia but in a more ad hoc, hit and miss fashion. But despite the considerable number of individually talented cricketers it has produced, rarely, as one of its best-loved captains the Nawab of Pataudi confesses, have 'they combined to make a composite team which could produce consistent performances over a period of years ... When Vijay Merchant or Gavaskar was flourishing, the middle order was brittle: when India had world class spinners there were no opening bowlers. And when Kapil Dev eventually turned up, the spinners had gone'.

It is just as well that an Indian prince should have made the point: cricket, a team game that allows the individual unbridled opportunites for glory should become in India a game where glorious individuals occasionally drag their team to odd moments of triumph. A prince needed to make that point for, in many ways, it is the legacy of the Indian princes' involvement with Indian cricket. The English had promoted the game in an ad hoc fashion: here a governor, there a viceroy, here a district official who particularly liked the game and wanted to see his Indian subjects take to it. The Indian response had come, initially, from the Parsees who, despite having lived in India for almost 1,300 years before the English arrived, understood, or thought they understood, the English sense of alienation in India and saw cricket as forging a bond between the Parsees, the old interlopers in India, and the English, the new interlopers. But what of the Indian princes? What of Ranji, surely here we have examples of a particular group of Indians, who had royal blood, promoting and organising cricket in India?

No writer of Indian cricket can ignore the princes, yet few, it seems, have bothered to study their effect on Indian cricket.

Adrian Murrell

Adrian Murrell

Adrian Murrell

Ranji (above left) is the English face of Indian cricket; Nayadu (above right) the Indian one. Though Ranji's English deeds are carefully re-told – mainly through Cardus – and the national championship named after him, Nayadu with his mixture of pride and stubbornness and a certain Indian arrogance, is seen as the father of Indian cricket. The memorial and its setting exemplifies a certain Indian obsession with ritualized honour: casting heroes in concrete at the first opportunity. Observe the surrounding park is unkempt, and the statue having been erected amidst ceremony, will languish there. What matters to Indians is the gesture of erecting the statue, not its upkeep.

Adrian Murrell

He has had various names: companions at Winchester and Oxford called him Noob, after Nawab of Pataudi, his princely title; he is now plain Mansur Ali Khan, but in Indian cricket everybody knows him as Tiger. Twelve years after his retirement he remains the most charismatic figure of the Indian game, his 'tigerish' qualities used to sell commercial products, and his pronouncements on the game listened to with deep respect. He was India's longest serving captain, and though by world standards his record was modest, in India he is seen as the man who revived the game. His present position illustrates the complex Indian response to an Indian Prince who learnt his cricket in England.

Patrick Eagar

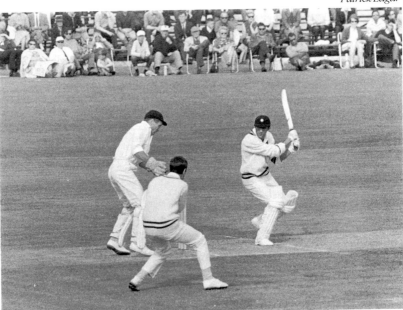

Patrick Eagar

Abbas Ali Baig (above) preceded Pataudi at Oxford, scored a century in his first Test at Old Trafford, was kissed by a girl at Brabourne Stadium in Bombay – after a second successive Test 50 – but virtually hounded out of the Test scene after his failures against Pakistan. Chandrasekhar (below) overcame the problems of a withered polio arm and the inconsistency of Indian selections to produce one of its most magical moments: victory against England at the Oval in 1971.

Patrick Eagar

Adrian Murrell

Patrick Eagar

As India defeated England in Bombay in December 1984 after 31 barren Tests, crowds exulted with anticipatory cries of 'Brownwash', hoping to repeat the West Indian 5–0 triumph over England. A few days later and less than 200 miles away in the hills, crowds in Pune were throwing bottles as India lost a one-day international. By the end of England's tour, much of India was thoroughly disenchanted with its cricket only to be revived by unexpected one-day successes in Australia. Indian crowds have always been fickle but since the World Cup triumph of 1983 crowds used to draws now expect victory at every turn and take defeats very bitterly.

Adrian Murrell

Non-paying customers watching the first ever one-day match played in India at Ahmedabad in 1981. Indian cricket experts confidently predicted that one-day cricket would never catch on; today it is the one form of cricket that does attract crowds disenchanted with the five-day variety. The growing sophistication of Indian urban life and television has a lot to do with this. Tests are televised live and many prefer to watch from the comfort of home, office, hotel or bar rather than endure the discomfort of stadiums. The aerials featured in the picture have become even more ubiquitous and Test cricket has suffered.

CAKE SUPPLY

All photos: Srenik Sett

Maidan cricket is the basis of the Indian game as these photographs taken during the rest day of the Calcutta Test between India and England in January 1985 illustrate. Calcutta's maidan is a vast central area of what passes for greenery in India: unkempt, chaotic but gratefully seized on by the city's Club cricketers. Almost every piece of the maidan is used even if square-leg is divided from mid-wicket by a filthy canal, or tea consist of dubious cakes from a tin box. The condition of the ground may not produce a Randall – would you dive across a canal? – but shades of David Gower and W. G. Grace can be seen.

Adrian Murrell

If one view sums up maidan cricket, then it is this. The proper Club match is at the Bombay Gymkhana where the first ever Test in India, against England, was played and which in the days of the Raj would not admit Indians as members. Now it does, but remains a snooty place keen to distance itself from the surrounding Indian chaos. The Victorian structure towering on the right is Victoria Terminus, Bombay's great railway station. Hidden by trees on the left is St Xavier's College, and next to it St Xavier's School where Gavaskar studied.

Virenchee Sagar, modern business patron, previously mentioned, who employs Gavaskar and a number of other Indian cricketers may be overstating the case when he accuses the Indian princes of retarding rather than promoting Indian cricket. But he has a point. Certainly for them, cricket and its promotion was more an outlet for intrigues, pomp and ambition in a troubled age, than a pleasure in promoting cricket for its own sake. Indian princes had a role to play in cricket. They did shape Indian cricket. It was not quite as beneficent and benevolent a role as it has been made out to be. Princely patronage, down the ages, has always had a touch of capriciousness, that is almost a princely prerogative. But if the princely patronage of Indian cricket came late, spasmodically and was motivated by political and social ambitions, it reflected individual princely fears and hopes about the future of princely India.

Princely India was unique. In 1929 a British committee reporting on princely India, the Report of the Indian States, 1928–9 (Cmd. 3302), said: 'It is generally agreed that the States are *sui generis*, that there is no parallel to their position in history, that they are governed by a body of convention and usage not quite like anything in the world'. So unique were they that British officials thought that the only historical parallel was provided by the position of the princes of the Holy Roman Empire at the beginning of the nineteenth century. And at one stage during the Raj the Indian Political Department prepared a memorandum on the unification of the German states which they hoped would provide some clues as to what would be the final position of princely India, once Britain withdrew from India. It has even been suggested that Mountbatten used this memorandum to convince the Indian princes to become part of India once the British had gone, but this seems somewhat unlikely.

Princely Indian was the most vivid illustration of the unique, one is inclined to say curious, nature of British rule in India. The British were supreme in India, but, as we have seen, they did not rule all of India. A third of the country was ruled by native Indian princes. Their relationship with the British government was defined by treaties of the eighteenth and early nineteenth centuries and fashioned by the slow, inexorable spread of British rule in India. Princely intrigue and endless machinations had opened the way for the British conquest of India. Treaties defined the relationship between the British Raj and those Indian princes, who, shrewdly realising the new power in India, came to terms with it. This was the doctrine of paramountcy. It was a British version of a fairly ancient Indian practice where Indian princes conceded certain powers to the dominant central ruler in return for rights and privileges. The princes recognised that the British were the paramount power in India with the princes enjoying – or claiming – sovereign status in the internal affairs of their own states.

This was the broad picture but there were many variations. Only about 40 of the 562 princes who made up princely India had treaties with the Crown and saw themselves as allies of the Crown, but resisted British interference in their internal affairs. Many of the princes were so small that they were no more than county squires and, in time, the British developed a theory of unlimited paramountcy of the Crown. Their supremacy, they argued, arose from their conquest of the country, not from any treaties they had signed with the princes, and it was this that was the source from which the princes derived their own internal sovereignty. Paramountcy was the subject of endless debate and discussion between the princes and the Raj. The British did intervene in the internal affairs of princes, and occasionally ousted a bad ruler. But, generally they allowed the princes to get on with their own internal affairs as long as they were loyal to the Crown. The British, buffeted by the growing tide of nationalism in India, found the princes an important bulwark against the democracy and change demanded by other Indians. Indeed, Viceroys aware of the need to use the princes to thwart the Indian nationalists, often drew back from pressing for internal reforms when faced with princely opposition.

The Raj in India was a mosaic of many interests. The British strategy was to ensure that enough of the interested groups supported them and helped neutralise the growing power of the nationalists. It was British attempts to appease the nationalists, after the First World War, that altered the princely perception of their place in the Raj and led to some of them patronising cricket. The first and most astounding thing about the Indian princes' involvement with cricket is that it came so late in the history of the Raj – and it prospered for no more than two decades. As Dr Richard Cashman has pointed out, it was not until the 1920s that Indian princes really took to cricket, and by the late 1940s the princely patrons had been replaced by businessmen and the bankers. Those two decades were years of princely political debate in India – they also saw the flourishing of princely money and the patronage of cricket. Political intrigue in the Chamber of Princes went hand in hand with patronage and intrigue on the cricketing field. The Raj's love for cricket was used as a lever to secure a better princely political position.

The statement by the Secretary of State for India in 1917 that India should work towards 'self-governing institutions' was a threat to the princes' power. The Chamber of Princes was a sop to soothe their fears. Its very structure was meant for what may be called the 'middle-class' prince – not small enough to be totally disregarded, but not really big enough to parlez directly with the British government. Thus of the Chamber's 120 members, not a single one represented the 327 rulers of tiny states who together ruled a population of just under one million. A further 127 states, which ruled eight million, had just twelve members. Only 108 princes enjoyed individual representation. Here again, and this point is crucial, it was the middling prince who really dominated the Chamber and the Standing Committee of seven princes which acted as the Chamber's executive. The middling Princes were:

Princely State	Population
Patiala	1.5 million
Bikaner	0.6 million
Alwar	0.7 million
Dholpur	0.23 million
Bhopal	0.7 million
Kutch	0.48 million
Nawanagar	0.34 million

These middling states had only 4.8 million of the 70 million people who were ruled by the Indian princes. The really great states of princely India – Hyderabad in the south with a population of 12.5 million and as big as France, Mysore with a population of 6 million, Cochin with a population of a million, Travancore with a population of 4 million, Baroda with a population of 2 million, Kolhapur with a population of 0.8 million, Jaipur with a population of 2.3 million, Jodhpur with a population of 1.8 million and Udaipur with a population of 1.4 million played no part in the Chamber's affairs. They were represented but that was nominal, they were big enough to argue their own case with the British and they resented any suggestion of parity with the lesser princes who dominated the Chamber.

Just as the bigger princes had no need for the Chamber, so they had no need for cricket. It was the middle-class princes calling the tune in the Chamber of Princes who also lavished their love and money on cricket.

Some of the larger States did promote cricket but, as in Hyderabad, this was the work of *jagirdars* – country squires – rather than of the ruler. The ruler of Hyderabad, the Nizam, said to be one of the richest, was also one of the meanest men in the world and his personal habits were so frugal that his parsimony became a legend. But he overcame this to become a great patron of arts and a keen scholar of languages such as Arabic, Persian, Hindi and Urdu. The game in Hyderabad developed because of Nawab Moin-Ud-Doula and Nawab Behram-Ud-Doula. Moin-Ud-Doula donated a gold cup named after him for an annual tournament which brought together the best players in the country as did his colleague, Nawab Behram-Ud-Doula. The Nizam cared little for cricket but it was these country squires, who owed their position to the Nizam, whose patronage encouraged the game in that state. Similar stories of minor aristocrats encouraging the game, either because they loved it, or because they saw it as a way of increasing their influence, formed part of the princely involvement with cricket in India. Thus Raja Dhanarajgiriji, another wealthy country squire, encouraged one of India's most colourful batsman, Mushtaq Ali; and Raja of Jath, who ruled a very small state of less than 100,000 people, imported Clarrie Grimmett to coach Vijay Hazere – one of India's great cricketers. Baroda, one of the heavyweight states, did come to cricket but not until the 1940s when the equation: *cricket patronage = political power* was no longer valid.

Statistics in cricket can mean a lot or nothing but the table on pages 90 and 91, which shows the princely states, their size and their influence in Indian cricket, is strikingly illustrative.

One prince who became a 'name' in cricket was the Maharaj Kumar of Vizianagram. Although he was classified as a prince and passed himself off as one, he was not really a prince. And though he played Test cricket for India, captained India in three Tests in England, he was no Test cricketer, or even a first-class cricketer. The title Maharaj Kumar, in a very subtle Indian princely way, suggested this. The normal title for a Hindu prince in India is

Maharaja, if he is a major prince, or Raja if he is a minor one. Muslim princes tend to have the title Nawab. Maharaj Kumar, literally, meant son of a prince – Kumar means young man – and the English equivalent would be the title of the Honourable for sons of peers who do not ascend to the title.

Vizianagram is a very small princely area in the southern state of Andhra Pradesh. Vizzy, as he was popularly known, did not succeed to the title, and had so much trouble with his nephew – who eventually did succeed – that he left his homeland to migrate to Benares in Uttar Pradesh, nearly a thousand miles away, to live on the Zamindara (landed estate) owned by the Vizianagram house. He was the classic case, as Indians put it, of the Maharaja of *Kuch bhi nahi* – meaning the Maharaja of nothing – and who did not do very much either! But he had a palace in Benares, which counted as a great status symbol, and a means to promote cricket. His private pitch on the palace grounds had E. H. Sewell, covering the MCC tour of India of 1933–4, in raptures – 'the appointments of the ground are well nigh perfect . . . the light is splendid. The white building of the palace, which is parallel to the pitch, and the sea green of the screen, both assisting to that end.' It was on this pitch that Douglas Jardine's team suffered their first, and only, defeat of the tour. Vizzy often recruited some of the leading players of the day for his team for a match, a season or even a tour. In 1930–1 he organised a tour of India and Ceylon to compensate for the cancellation of the MCC tour and persuaded Jack Hobbs and Herbert Sutcliffe – neither being readily open to persuasion – to join his team. In 1934 Constantine was brought to India. Vizzy never persuaded Donald Bradman to join his team but made a film of Bradman giving Vizzy batting lessons after the Oval test of 1930, and proudly told Indians that 'films of these lessons have been taken and these will be shown whenever necessary and any little batting fault is corrected'. Cynical Indians couldn't help thinking that Vizzy's own batting had so many faults that not even the great Bradman could have corrected them. Players who went on Vizzy's tours did not receive money to protect their amateur status, but many gifts including clothes replete with gold buttons and the Vizianagaram crest, a silver statuette of a batsman, trophies and, often, cash purses at the end of the tour.

Had Vizzy been content with that he would have had a position in Indian cricket similar to the one occupied, and at about the same time, by Sir Julian Cahn – a man in love with the game using

Princely States – Patronage and Effect

Name of Princely State	Size in Square Miles	Population (1931)	Test Player	Cricket Specialisation	Captaincy
NORTHERN INDIA					
Patiala	5,932	1,625,520	Yuvraj of Patiala	Batsman	Captain (unofficial test)
Jammu and Kashmir	85,884	3,646,243	–	–	–
Pataudi	53	18,873	Iftikhar Ali Pataudi	Batsman	Captain
			Mansur Ali Khan Pataudi	Batsman	Captain
RAJASTAN					
Udaipur (Mewar)	12,915	1,566,910	–	–	–
Banswara	1,606	225,106	Hanumant Singh	Batsman	–
Dungarpur	1,447	227,544	–	–	–
WESTERN INDIA					
Baroda	8,135	2,443,007	D. K. Gaekwad	Batsman	Captain
			A. D. Gaekwad	Batsman	–
Kolhapur	3,217	957,137	J. M. Ghorparde	Batsman	–
Junagadh	3,337	545,152	–	–	–
Nawanagar	3,791	409,192	K. S. Ranjitsinhji	Batsman	–
			K. S. Duleepsinhji	Batsman	–
			K. S. Indrajitsinh	Wicket keeper	–
Jath	909	90,102	–	–	–
Porbandar	642	115,673	–	–	–

Limbdi	344	40,080	Yajurvindra Singh	Batsman	—
Bilka	167	45,000	—	—	—
Wadhawan	243	42,602	—	—	—
CENTRAL INDIA					
Gwalior	26,383	3,523,070	—	—	—
Indore	9,570	1,318,217	—	—	—
Bhopal	6,902	729,555	—	—	—
Dewas Senior	449	83,321	—	—	—
Alirajpur	836	101,963	—	—	—
BENGAL					
Cooch Behar	1,318	590,886	—	—	—
SOUTHERN INDIA					
Hyderabad (Nawab Moin-Ul-Doula)	82,698	14,436,148	—	—	—
Vizianagram	—	276,533	Maharaj Kumar of Vizianagram	Batsman	Captain
(Zamindari Lands, UP)	21	—			

Source: Dr Richard Cashman, *Players, Patrons and Crowds.*

his money and influence to promote and encourage it. But for Vizzy the other side of patronage was personal ambition – a common failing with most Indian princes. Patrons need not be altruistic but when their munificence is laced with such deadly ambition, the results can be very serious. So it was the Vizzy. Vizzy, with a donation of 50,000 rupees, had helped underwrite the 1932 tour which included India's first ever Test at Lord's. Four years later India returned to England hoping to build on that first experience. Despite losing the 1932 Lord's Test, India's per-formance had been creditable and left the impression of much hope for the future. But the 1936 tour had barely got under way before such hopes were cruelly dashed, and by the end of it Indian cricket was in a turmoil – the international consequences of which continued to taint it for many a decade. Vizzy was at the very centre of the turmoil. The 1932 Indian team had been led by the Maharaja of Porbandar. This was Indians mimicking the British cricket division between amateurs and professionals. In English cricket an amateur, whatever his playing merits, was always Captain. In India it was felt that the Captain of the cricket team ought to be a prince. But Porbandar was sensible enough to realise that while socially he made a very acceptable Captain, as a cricketer he was not up to much. So at the Test match C. K. Nayudu, probably India's greatest cricketer, captained the side. Keeping up with the Joneses also tends to be a princely habit – at least in India – and long before the 1936 tour Vizzy had set out his stall to acquire the captaincy. In fact he had been appointed as Deputy Vice-Captain – a post that almost defies description – on the 1932 tour but had withdrawn with the rather mysterious claim that he was 'making this immense sacrifice for the sake of the future of cricket in India'. To cynics this had sounded like Vizzy doubletalk to cover up his disappointment that he was only number three in the side, next to two other princes, a position that hurt his ego. So in 1936 he wished to take no chances.

The full story of how Vizzy became Captain of the 1936 tour may never be told so enmeshed is it in princely politics of the time. But an outline is possible, and instructive. It began, amazingly, two years before the tour when the Nawab of Pataudi Senior returned to India. The son-in-law of the Nawab of Bhopal, whose influence on the Indian Board matched that in the Chamber of Princes, Pataudi was a clear front runner to lead India. Although he had made his debut for India against Australia on Jardine's Bodyline tour, scoring a century in his first Test, but being dropped subsequently, Pataudi now declared himself ready to play for India. Indian cricket seemed to have found its saviour. Ranji couldn't play for India, since India didn't have a Test team then and many Indians commented caustically on Duleep's preference for England over India. Pataudi's belated acceptance of India over-joyed them. On 29 October 1934 Pataudi was voted Captain of the Indian team to tour England in 1936, beating his opponent C. K. Nayudu by a handsome margin – Nayudu got only four votes. Long term is a good thing but this was still an amazing decision. The tour was eighteen months away. Pataudi was known to be in indifferent health, it had broken down during both the 1933 and the 1934 English seasons. Why then was he appointed Captain eighteen months in advance? Perhaps euphoria had got the better of the Indians, though, the cynical explanation that emerged later was that it was meant to pave the way for Vizzy to become Captain.

It is hard to deny this cynicism. As the months went on Pataudi's health did not improve and, some months before the tour, he withdrew citing his health as the reason. Many doubted this and some of his friends later told an Indian cricket writer that he had withdrawn 'for reasons of state'. For reasons of Vizzy is more like it; Pataudi had served his purpose as a stalking horse for Vizzy. In 1934 had Vizzy been proposed as Captain, in place of Nayudu, he would have stood little or no earthly chance. Pataudi with the glamour of his having played for England could easily beat Nayudu. And with Nayudu defeated, Vizzy could now spin his web of captaincy intrigue.

Vizzy may have been a poor cricketer but off the field he was a shrewd politician. The federal structure of the country meant regional imbalance and Vizzy shrewdly promised disaffected state associations better representation in the Indian team. A selector and respected former cricketer Dr Kanga had already resigned on grounds of 'princely interference', and there was the intriguing presence of Major Brittain-Jones, who for some bizarre reason was representing Rajputana on the Indian Board. Behind these men was Lord Willingdon, Viceroy in India, who was a friend of Vizzy and like all British administrators saw the princes as a bulwark against the rising tide of nationalism. He was keen to have his man as Captain in England. The result was one of the strangest teams ever to leave on a cricket tour. Vizzy was appointed Captain and there was no Vice-Captain and no Tour

Selection Committee. All the decisions rested with Vizzy, assisted by Major Brittain-Jones, who became the Manager. The price of political lobbying is bloated cricket teams and the Indians finally comprised twenty-one players. It was not so much a team as a prince's retinue; Vizzy, travelling with 'thirty six items of personal luggage and two servants'.

Picture the scene. Vizzy, a plumpish, rather hunched figure, perpetually standing in the slips and peering through spectacles at a game he did not seem to understand. With reason one is inclined to add. England not only marked his debut as a Captain of India, but also his debut in first-class cricket. The matches in India he had taken part in were not by English standards first class, and he was yet to play in the Ranji trophy, the Indian equivalent of the county championship. In the past, when he had captained his own team in matches in India, he had used the experience of players like Nayudu to help set the field, or change the bowling. In England helpful suggestions of that nature from Vizzy's team mates, and even in the English press, seemed to incense him. Vizzy's reaction was to be even more capricious and this was to lead to the tour's great explosion. Lala Amarnath who had made a spectacular century on his debut against Jardine's England team two years previously in India, had shown much promise on the tour. He had scored over 600 runs and taken 32 wickets. But in a minor counties game Amarnath, padded up and ready to bat, found himself waiting while others lower down the batting order were promoted. His reaction was strong, characteristically Punjabi and, no doubt, he was rather rude about Vizzy and his captaincy. All this was faithfully reported back to the prince who, egged on by Major Brittain-Jones, and perhaps, Lord Willingdon, decided that Amarnath had to be sent home.

India's cricket historians are still divided about who really showed Amarnath the red card. Was it Vizzy? Or was it Major Brittain-Jones? One theory, perhaps suffering a bit from latter-day nationalist revisionism, states that it was Major Brittain-Jones who really wanted Amarnath sent home. As a member of Lord Willingdon's staff, he treated the Indians as people belonging to a subject country. He, so the theory goes, had every reason 'to magnify the Amarnath episode for political gains in order to prove to the world that even a few Indian cricketers couldn't live as a team, let alone a whole nation'. The Government of India Act 1935 had just been enacted and Indians were being given greater powers, but such public displays of disunity in an Indian cricket team playing in England could be a handy weapon to use to answer Indian nationalists' cry for more freedom. If Indians couldn't manage a cricket team, how could they manage a whole country? Perhaps the nationalist cricket historians are right, though, one suspects, that if Major Brittain-Jones did the stirring, Vizzy and some of his cohorts were willing to be easily stirred.

The scenes that followed have a fictional touch about them. According to A. S. de Mello, an Indian administrator, demonstrations were planned in Bombay to greet Amarnath returning from England and de Mello had to 'kidnap' Amarnath, by smuggling him aboard the pilot launch before the ship docked and keeping him under cover at a hotel. Amarnath denies this colourful story, though his sending off led to a committee of enquiry headed by the then Chief Justice of the Bombay High Court, Sir John Beaumont. The Beaumont enquiry felt that the action against Amarnath was too severe and stern. As for Vizzy his performance at social functions where he was 'brilliantly successful' was noted but the committee found that his batting was below Test standard and that 'he did not understand the placing of the team or the changing of the bowling, and never maintained any regular order in batting'.

The committee had got it just about right. Vizzy was knighted during the tour but the tour was a disaster. But if the Beaumont enquiry meant the end of Vizzy's playing career, the cricket-politician in him never gave up and for the next three decades, until his death, his hand and his purse pursued many a scheme, doing some good but wrecking many plans.

In the process he sustained a princely legacy that has continued to haunt Indian cricket. A legacy of unbridled individualism, which could often be destructive, of sudden caprice followed by sudden munificence, of charming generosity destroyed by wilful malice, and a game which was meant to combine the highest of individual talents and the noblest of team spirits, converted into an exotic display of individual arrogance. Some flavour of this can be found in this description by H. G. Wickham, a member of the northern Indian police service between 1904–22, of the Maharaja of Kashmir at play:

At 3 o'clock in the afternoon the Maharaja himself would come down to the Ground, the band would play the Kashmir anthem, salaams were made and he then went off to a special tent where he sat for a time, smoking his long water-pipe. At 4.30 or thereabouts he decided he would bat. It didn't matter which side was batting, his own team or ours. He was padded by two attendants and gloved by two more. Somebody carried his bat and he walked to the wicket looking very dignified but very small and with an enormous turban upon his head. In one of the matches I happened to be bowling and my first ball hit his stumps, but the wicket keeper quick as lightning called 'No Ball' and the match went on. The only way that the Maharaja could get out was by lbw. And after fifteen or twenty minutes batting he said he felt tired and he was duly given out lbw. What the scorer did about his innings, which was never less than half a century, goodness only knows.

The eccentric Maharaja is not always destructive. The house of Patiala was India's most beneficent princely patron. Yet Rajendra Singh, who started the cricket tradition at Patiala, took to the game because he was bored. In the nineteenth century, like all Indian princes, Rajendra Singh had taken a keen interest in polo and pig-sticking. The early 1890s had seen Rajendra Singh's polo team win the Punjab Polo cup four times, the Simla-based Beresford cup three times with his horses winning two viceroy's cups and four civil service cups. The year 1895 saw a marvellous victory over the rival royal house of Jodhpur in the Punjab tournament and this seems to have satiated Rajendra Singh's appetite. He required a new challenge and took to cricket. Within three years the Patiala Eleven was one of the best in the country, consisting of Ranji, English professionals like Jack Herd, the Middlesex bowler, W. Brockwell, the Surrey batsman and Arthur Priestly, MP for Grantham, friend of Ranji and a decent enough amateur cricketer. In addition to these, the Patiala team had several very good Indian players including the leading player K. M. Mistri.

Rajendra Singh's impact on cricket was great. The Patiala team set a standard that others followed. Rajendra Singh's son, Bhupinder Singh, successfully combined cricketing pleasures with other pleasures. He surrounded himself with several hundred wives and concubines and his palace included a scented swimming pool. He often went to bat in bright pink and blue turbans adorned with expensive pearl earrings. Once when he was playing for the MCC one of the earrings was lost and play was held up for several minutes. Bhupinder, like most cricketing princes, used cricket to promote his politics and vice versa. And like his father he too brought out leading English professionals to India, George Hurst, Wilfred Rhodes, Maurice Leyland, Harold Larwood and the Australian-born Frank Tarrant. In many ways Bhupinder Singh went further than his father. Rajendra Singh had concentrated mostly on cricket in Patiala, Bhupinder organised, financed and captained the 1911 tour of an Indian team to England, helped establish the Indian Board of Control, donated money for pavilions and trophies, including the Ranji trophy, and did much to encourage the game. His son, the Yuvraj of Patiala was probably one of the finest cricketers to play for India – albeit in unofficial Tests – and had he had some relish for the cricketing intrigues so intrinsically part of Indian cricket he might well have been the Captain of the ill-fated 1936 tour. A tall, hard-hitting batsman, the Yuvraj seemed to combine both the batting dash associated with cricketing princes – his grandfather once scored twenty-one runs in just eight and a half minutes – and the chivalry which is the hallmark of any prince. In one of the unofficial Tests that he played in, the Yuvraj, coming in with the score at sixty-six for four, hit five 6s and one 4 in just thirty minutes. It could not prevent the Indians from being soundly beaten but it embellished the princely legend of batting.

Although Bhupinder, like his father, did a great deal for Indian cricket, inevitably his cricketing and political interests clashed. Often while he was immersed in politics, coaches would find they had nothing to do but kill time. They would lose interest in cricket coaching and drift away in disgust. Perhaps the whole nature of princely patronage of Indian cricket and its consequences would have been different had Ranji played a part in it. But he didn't and it is his legacy that is the most difficult for Indian cricket.

Of Ranji's place in cricket there can be no conceivable doubt. In the *The complete Who's Who of Test Cricketers*, Ranji is the legendary prince who 'brought Eastern magic to the cricket fields of England, America and Australia'. And his latest biographer, Alan Ross, is convinced that Ranji is one of only half a dozen in the history of the game who have added something new to it. 'His true memorial is in the memory of those who saw him, transmitted down the generations: a shiver of the spine at Hove or Lord's, the air fined with that latest of late cuts, that silkiest of glances. The

Indian Prince, in all his finery, abroad in an English summer.' **Ranji** was a giant in the golden age of cricket – indeed his deeds, and his cricketing style and genius, made the golden age. But that was an English golden age of cricket. How much of an Indian prince was he? What could he do for Indian cricket?

Alan Ross accepts that Ranji was alienated from Indian cricket. His biography ends with two postscripts. The first of these assesses Ranji's contribution to the game, the second presents what is called 'An Indian View'. The Indian view is that of Anthony de Mello, one of India's great cricket administrators and a founder of the Indian Board of Control. Writing in a portrait of Indian sport in 1959 de Mello bluntly states:

> Ranji did absolutely nothing for Indian sport and sportsmen. To all our requests for aid, encouragement and advice, Ranji gave but one answer: Duleep and I are English cricketers. He could not have been more blunt. In short, Ranji was a different man in England than in India . . . In most other walks of life he was a model Indian Prince. But the Ranji who settled in Jamnagar after the First World War was an all together different man from the great cricketer who delighted English crowds in earlier years . . . it is understandable that when he finally left England to live in India he should leave something behind him. There was talk too of an unhappy love affair; and certainly as an Indian Prince Ranji could not have married an English girl. If true, it would take us a step nearer to the explanation why Ranji left his heart somewhere among the green fields of England.

De Mello, while acknowledging Ranji's work in Nawanagar, is scathing about Popsey the 'ironic, bitter parrot, who seemed closer to him than any man'. De Mello concluded that 'towards the end of his life, he gave the impression that he was disillusioned', waiting for something he knew he would never have. Ross suggests extenuating circumstances. Ranji came into cricketing prominence when there was no Indian cricket at Test level, or for that matter, at national level. All his serious cricket was played in England and, inevitably, he was happiest with the friends he had made in the formative period of his cricketing life. But something more than this mere recital of historical facts is necessary to understand de Mello's expression of Ranji's alienation. Perhaps Ranji's bachelor status really was because he was pining for a lost girl in England. Indian princes, as de Mello said, were, indeed, discouraged from marrying English girls. Whether Ranji had a lost love or not we shall never know. Alan Ross, so eloquent about Ranji's cricket and his role as a prince, is mysteriously silent about his private life. We are not told why Ranji never married or, if, indeed, there was an English love in his life. De Mello's insinuation is quoted, but not explained – cricketing biographies tend to be reticent on such subjects! The point is important with respect to Ranji because of the way de Mello and other Indians read into this the cause of Ranji's decision to do nothing for Indian cricket.

But 'nothing' is perhaps rather a strong word. De Mello is not a disinterested witness and Ranji did play cricket very regularly in India until 1915 when his duties as ruler of Nawanagar took precedence. He shared cricket coaches with other states and in unobtrusive ways encouraged youngsters to play, he was the first to observe the potential of one of India's finest fast bowlers Amarsingh. Perhaps Ranji felt it was enough to set a wonderful example by his personal deeds – propagating, as Alan Ross puts it, 'the idea of Ranji, the awareness that it was an Indian who had become the greatest batsman in the world'. Certainly this idea of Ranji exercised a powerful influence on Indian minds. Even today school children in India read with delight and wonder Neville Cardus's marvellous essay on Ranji as told in a probably apocryphal story of the Yorkshire bowler Ted Wainwright. Every year Yorkshire would come down to Hove, the moist air would be heavy, Wainwright would grab a couple of early wickets and then Ranji and Fry would get together and by the end of the day the score would be 300 for 2. This essay was part of our school syllabus and certainly the idea of Ranji, the Indian, dominating Yorkshire, the might of England, had a great effect on us. However, Ross may be exaggerating slightly when he said that this 'contributed more than anything else to the Indian cricketer's realisation of his own possibilities'.

The more relevant question is 'Did Ranji ever consider himself an Indian?' I do not mean it in the sense that de Mello and Ross do, of Ranji considering himself an English cricketer as opposed to an Indian one. I mean did he consider himself an Indian as I consider myself an Indian, or the editor of this book Derek Wyatt considers himself English? This is not as arcane as it may sound. It goes to the very heart of Ranji's legacy. Ranji, said John Lord in *The Maharajas* was, 'the first Indian of any kind to become universally known and popular'. But if Ranji did not consider himself to be an Indian, the sentence has no meaning, or a very different one from what the writer intends. In fact Ranji's alleged 'Indianness' has suffered such a curious metamorphosis that in Scyld Berry's *Cricketwallah* Ranji, amazingly, appears as an Indian nationalist fighting the British for Indian independence. According to Berry, Ranji, while Chancellor in the Chamber of Princes, had a serious disagreement with the Viceroy over India's future. 'Although English in many ways and loyal to the Crown, Ranji wanted independence for India far sooner than the British planned. A few days after this disagreement in New Delhi, he returned to Jamnagar, and died in his bedroom of heart failure'. There was indeed a disagreement, and Ranji did die a few days later but to read into this Ranji the nationalist opposing the bureaucratic Raj is certainly overdoing things.

Ranji, though born in India, was not Indian but Rajput. Roland Wild, who Ranji chose to be his biographer, is eloquent about Ranji's ancestry. The eloquence concentrates on the Rajput race, their ability to trace the clan back through centuries, their ancient pedigree. Throughout Wild's biography, published in 1934, a year after Ranji's death, there is much about Ranji the Rajput but nothing about Ranji the Indian. Ranji's loyalties were to his state, Nawanagar, to his people in Nawanagar and to the King Emperor. Though Nawanagar was too small to have a Treaty of Accession to the Crown, Ranji, like all princes in India, saw a personal link between rule in Nawanagar and the King Emperor's rule over the British Empire. The idea of an Indian nation, let alone one free of British rule, must have struck Ranji as quite absurd.

The background to the dispute between Ranji and the Viceroy centred around the British Government's plans to introduce a new method of ruling India. Although the new proposals offered only the slightest concession to Indian nationalism, the princes refused to accept the new scheme and it was never implemented. Ranji, as Chancellor of the Chamber of Princes, was actively involved in formulating princely opinion. In July 1931, addressing an all party meeting of MPs in the House of Commons, Ranji made it abundantly clear that he was 'absolutely opposed ... to all this talk of independence'. He and the princes would favour federation provided there were safeguards for the way the princes ran their own states. Later when the meeting of the Chambers of

100

Princes took place in New Delhi on Monday 20 March 1933, Ranji made it clear that he did not support the British scheme for a federation of states. 'I have nothing but the friendliest and the most brotherly of sentiments for British India and I wish her leaders well. I hope that she will attain her aspirations, but I hope she will do this without involving the States.'

This is not the voice of an Indian nationalist urging independence from Britain. It is the voice of a prince who keenly felt his Rajput, Hindu origins and who was desperately worried that even the limited reforms the British were introducing in India would damage the ancient rights of kings. Ranji, though a benevolent, far-sighted ruler, was no democrat. He was an autocrat and his autocracy derived its power and authority from what he believed to be his Rajput inheritance. It was 1933, Hitler was about to come to power in Germany, fascism was on the march and democracy seemed a poor bet. Ranji, a rather proud Rajput, would no more have advocated independence for India than he would have renounced his Rajput inheritance. This is not to make a charge against Ranji. He was merely reflecting the princely ideas and attitudes of the time. So if Ranji did not do much for Indian cricket it is because he did not think of India as a cricketing nation. He did not think of India as a cricketing nation because he could not conceive of India as a political nation. India as a political nation was born fourteen years after Ranji died and, had he lived, as his successors' actions show, he would have undoubtedly opposed it. He advised Duleep to play for England rather than India and he did so because to him an Indian team meant nothing. Had Nawanagar managed to get together a Test team then, I am sure, Ranji would have advised Duleep to play for Nawanagar. For in as much as a king is ever a nationalist, Ranji was a Nawanagar nationalist. He was, perhaps, a Rajput nationalist, if that term can have any meaning. He was not an Indian nationalist and to accuse him, as de Mello does, and other Indians do, of not doing much for Indian cricket is to miss the point.

CHAPTER 6

The Besieged Hero

Every country gets the hero it deserves. It is difficult to imagine John McEnroe as anything other than an American hero. According to Professor Jack Higgs, while he is not yet a national hero, he is as thoroughly American as the New York Yankees. In India there are heroes and there are Gods. In the West the two terms, at least in popular usage, may be interchangeable but in India they have rather distinct meanings.

The ideal Hindu God is Rama, that wonderfully self-effacing person who, in order to keep his father's word, was ready to sacrifice his kingdom, and in order to please his subjects, was ready to sacrifice his ideal wife. Ramayana is one of the great classics of our times, though I don't suppose any Western child knows the story, but that is a reflection of the effects of colonialism. In India and South East Asia its status is far higher than that enjoyed by Homer's *Iliad* in the West.

In this great Hindu myth Rama is God incarnated as man – the eldest son of a king who reigns at Ayodhya. He is about to succeed his father when the distressed king summons Rama. Some years ago, cherished back to health and life by his second wife after a war wound, he had made extravagant promises to her. She was now cashing in her chips. The second wife wanted her son, Rama's stepbrother, to become king. Rama the perfect man immediately understands and, with his wife and another brother, he vanishes into the forest to start fourteen years of exile. The story of Ramayana is actually the years of exile; the tribulations of Sita, Rama's wife, who is kidnapped, then rescued and the eventual, joyous return of Rama to Ayodhya.

Ramayana does tend to come overloaded with self-effacing heroes. The stepbrother for whom Rama vacated the throne refused to actually sit on it. Through those fourteen years he sits in front of the throne that Rama was supposed to have occupied, using a pair of Rama's shoes as a symbol of the lost king. Ramayana is a story of good triumphing over evil – and there are some marvellously evil characters in it – and its moral is not lost in contemporary Indian life. Rama's portrait stares down from a million Indian *pan* shops, he is the ideal Hindu and when he reigned there was perfection on earth. It was Mahatma Gandhi's political aim to recreate Ramrajya (rule of Rama) in India.

But Indians distinguish between Rama, as the great political God-hero and the more modern heroes. Indians, even if they cannot speak a word of English, actually use the English word 'hero' and when they do so they are thinking of the hero in Hindi films. While occasionally Hindi films do have heroes full of excessive goodness, such as Rama, a hero in the Indian film world, and as understood by most Indians in contemporary India, is a somewhat rakish individual. He probably has a lock of hair perpetually falling across his eyes, which he constantly brushes back, either with his fingers or with a dainty comb he keeps in his hip pocket. His clothes are just that bit too fashionable, his manner just that bit too outlandish, he is both a bit of a voyeur and a bit of a poser. The Hindi film world hero can, sometimes, be something of a character. In fact Indians can hurl the word hero as an abuse, or at least a reproach. If somebody fails whilst trying something outlandish, or ends up looking stupid, it is not unusual for his friend or colleague to say 'What do you think you are doing? Trying to be a hero?' Heroes are difficult to live with. In India there is a problem in that while it would prefer all its heroes to be like Rama, it often finds that they are a caricature of the Hindi film hero – slightly more lewd, slightly fatter, slightly more absurd and a lot less lovable. The contradiction between the ideal and reality is always going to cause problems. Problems clearly illustrated in the way Indians react to Sunil Gavaskar, India's greatest bat and one of the finest in the world.

Gavaskar's place in cricket can hardly be in doubt. He has now scored more centuries than Donald Bradman and more runs than anybody else in Test cricket. He has done so opening the innings for a country whose batting has often been very brittle; he has gone out to bat knowing he could echo Louis XIV and say, 'After me, the deluge of wickets.' He burst on the Test scene in 1971, aged just 21 and with a handful of first-class matches behind him, scoring 774 runs in his first Test series – against Sobers's West Indians. It was a Bradman-like opening and if his subsequent series haven't quite matched the first, he has been remarkably consistent producing runs in the sort of profusion that has not been seen before in Indian cricket, and rarely elsewhere. Gavaskar returned from that West Indies trip as a celebrity, or as Indians like to put it a VIP, a Very Important Person. The extent of Indian adulation for a VIP produces wondrous gasps in England, and Gavaskar has been subjected to hero worship almost from the beginning.

He receives some eighty letters a day, even his teenage son receives letters, and Sunil's *darshan* is eagerly sought. Literally the word means 'introduction', but in India it has a quasi-mystical association with crowds gathering to be near a great man or woman. Thus Mrs Gandhi regularly had crowds gathering in front of her house every morning hoping to catch her darshan. If Gavaskar, say, is going shopping in a Bombay street, soon after he enters a shop, word passes through the street, that the great man is around. Crowds, in that characteristic Indian fashion, gather as if from nowhere. They want nothing from him, not even his autograph; all they want is to be near him, and, perhaps, be touched by his magic. Film stars and politicians have always enjoyed such darshan, but Gavaskar was one of the first modern Indian cricketers to do so. At times the swarm of crowds, say at railway stations, has been such that his son and wife have had to drop out of the wrong side of the carriage and escape across the tracks.

But this adulation comes mixed with unease, disquiet and downright hostility. English writers, like Dudley Doust, have misinterpreted the adulation as uncritical hero worship. Gavaskar is no Rama, nor, perhaps, a Hindi film hero. The Indian response to him is complex, reflecting both pride and unease: wonder about his achievements but doubt about the means he has used to attain his ends. Here is how Mansur Ali Khan Pataudi in an article entitled *The Decline of Indian Cricket*, puts the case against Gavaskar:

> Gavaskar was the greatest, and while no one doubted this, it is plain that only some Bombay players payed him sycophantic homage. Perhaps the others were jealous but no matter how hard he tried, many cricketers from elsewhere were unable to give him their full trust (Dilip Doshi is an example). They felt that Gavaskar stood for Gavaskar though he had often clashed with the authorities for the benefit of his team.

Pataudi's explanation for the unease Indians feel about Gavaskar is money. Prize money came into India in 1969. Pataudi was Captain at a team meeting when Wadehar, who was to replace him later, suggested that it be shared. Pataudi spent two years in legal fees to convince the income tax department that the money ought not to be taxed and the Indian off-spinner Venkataraghavan was given the task of ensuring that the prize money was properly split between the various players. Pataudi said that was not only because he was honest 'but he had the knack of dividing thousands by any number and arriving at an even figure'. Later Venkataraghavan's position as team accountant was to be taken by Chetan Ghauhan, and it was partly his departure from the team that contributed to the hassles about sharing prize money in later years. According to Pataudi:

> Gavaskar opened up entire new vistas of making money. He had noticed how quickly cricketers once out of limelight were actually shunned by the same people who had fussed over them, fought for the pleasure of inviting them home and queued to have photographs taken with them. In Bombay only money seemed to matter, and there was more than one way to make it. Gavaskar found them all. Advertising, film producing (this may have been for a lark), writing articles (on the same match but for different publications), taking a fee for organising matches, writing instant books, which were spiced to sell better, appearance money (one paid for the pleasure of entertaining the team) and signing contracts with the manufacturers of sports equipment. He became the first Indian millionaire through cricket, rich enough to buy a flat in the centre of Bombay. In a capitalist cricketing country he would have been considered a financial genius. In India they began to call him a mercenary, and within the team he became the envy of some who felt that their contribution to Indian cricket was not being fully appreciated. Why should Gavaskar hog all the publicity as well as the money? The answer was simple: he had reached those dizzy heights to which no Indian cricketer in his right mind would even dream of aspiring. As importantly, he was articulate where others were dumb, he was controversial where others dared not to be, he could even be witty and this made him ideal material for the media and the advertiser.

Pataudi, as ever, has got to the nub of the problem. For many Indians Sunil Gavaskar is 'money-mad'. Almost everyone describes his actions, from his flirtation with Kerry Packer's world series cricket, his appearance at some social function or the other, to his supposed lust for money. By any international cricket standards, let alone the standards of tennis or golf, Gavaskar is extremely poorly paid. He only earns something like £35,000 a year, some £5,000 less than what Ian Botham earns from his bat contract alone. But £35,000 is a lot of money in India – and much more than that earned by cricketers in the pre-Gavaskar era. Gavaskar's crime is that he does not accept the Indian dichotomy about money.

It has always surprised me to find certain Westerners depicting the Indians as a uniquely non-materialistic people, not interested in this world, or its worldly goods, but only in a sort of mystical after-life. *Maya,* illusion, the West believes, is a central Indian plank. It may be a central Indian, or rather Hindu, philosophical belief but the idea that Indians are not materialistic is absurd. India is probably the most materialistic place on earth. The Hindu belief in a pantheon of Gods enables them to worship many Gods. One of the most popular, and worshipped with great fervour, is Lakshmi, the Goddess of Wealth. Perhaps the most celebrated temple in Bombay, certainly the most popular is *Mahalakshmi,* where a wonderous statue of Lakshmi is worshipped every day with milk, ghee, money, and various other offerings. The different Hindu communities have their different Gods, but almost all of them have an annual Lakshmi Puja which is marked with great devotion and enthusiasm.

The confusion in the West arises from the fact that while Indians are terribly materialistic, they do not flaunt their materialism. They do not like bragging about how much money they have, or how many cars they possess, or about their lifestyle. Indians hunger for money, perhaps more than most, but they do not like their heroes to openly proclaim this.

Gavaskar possesses another un-Indian characteristic – in cricket he is very consistent. The same could not be said for the true Rama-like figure in Indian cricket – a definite contrast to Gavaskar. While it is hard to see Gavaskar vacating the crease at any time – let alone in order to redeem someone else's promise – one could imagine Viswanath doing so. He is the Rama of Indian cricket. Physically both Gavaskar and Viswanath look similar – both small men – and they made their impact at roughly the same time. Viswanath, in fact, made his debut in 1969 scoring a century in his first Test; before the West Indies tour of 1971 began, it was

Viswanath who was considered the main batsman. But on the tour he suffered an injury, Gavaskar made his debut and while Viswanath came back he never quite recaptured the spotlight. Indians have always debated the merits of these two batsmen. Gavaskar, himself, generously admits that Viswanath is the greater batsman. 'I have just one stroke to every ball, he seems to have four or five.' It makes Viswanath so cherishable, so lovable, but like all the great Indian heroes, he is fallible. A Viswanath's innings can be an innings of great joy, but it can also mount to nothing. It allows Indians much speculation on their favourite subject of 'what if . . .' Viswanath accepts whatever is given to him modestly and with the sort of self-effacing air that Hindus find so charming.

But despite Viswanath's charm and the evident understanding between the two men the Gavaskar and Viswanath argument can generate extreme passion amongst their supporters. I witnessed one such scene as Sunil was making his memorable 221 against England at the Oval in 1979.

The Oval then had its cramped, almost subterranean, press box; here I sat next to an Indian journalist. As Sunil slowly built the Indian innings, and turned what looked like a hopeless defeat into the most glorious victory, my Indian colleague was dismissive of his efforts. Sunil, he declared, had never really faced proper bowling. He had made his runs when the top bowler of the opposing side had been absent. Sometime earlier on that last day Hendrick, England's most difficult bowler, had limped away. My friend pointed to this as confirmation of his thesis. Even Sunil reaching his century, then his double century, then placing India on what looked like the high road to victory, did not dampen his anti-Sunil tirade. Set 438 India now needed just a few runs for victory and, with a few overs left, a remarkable five-day test had turned into a limited overs run chase. Kapil Dev, promoted in the order, got out and Viswanath strode to the wicket. My friends nudged me and said 'what you have seen so far is nothing, here comes God. He will take us to victory.'

As it happened Sunil got out soon afterwards, Viswanath got a rather dodgy decision and India just failed to win the match that had looked theirs for the taking, by nine runs. I was sorely tempted to mock my Indian colleague about his God, but I resisted that. But such are the passions that Sunil arouses that even after that great innings, there were whispers in some Indian quarters that he had got out because he didn't want India to win.

On that tour India was being captained by Venkat, who had supplanted Sunil, Captain for the previous home series, because of Sunil's flirtation with Kerry Packer's world cricket series. Immediately after the Oval Test, the Indians flew home to face the Australians and on the plane, with the sort of subtlety that has made the Indian selectors famous, it was announced by the pilot that Venkat had been replaced as Captain by Sunil. Immediately the rumours began to circulate. Yes, of course, Sunil played a great innings, but why didn't he carry it to completion? Why didn't he ensure that India had won? Well, said the anti-Sunil brigade, the reason is that his 221 was a personal effort. It impressed his unique mark on English cricket where he hadn't scored as heavily as elsewhere, but it was just short of clinching victory for India. A victory for India would have meant a victory for Venkat, and the Indian selectors could hardly have dropped Venkat after that.

This is, of course, an absolutely disgraceful suggestion. He played the innings with a throbbing toothache, although physical pain of that type always seems to spur him on. When, after eight hours and nine minutes he finally got out, he was a very tired man. It would have been fantastic if he had actually made the winning hit against England, but to blame a man after such a stupendous achievement seems extraordinary. It is also characteristic of certain Indian attitudes, certainly an anti-Sunil Gavaskar attitude, that out of such personal success they could construct a conspiracy. It explains the passion Sunil Gavaskar arouses, passions that Fritzy would have understood, though not necessarily condoned.

We must, indeed, look to Fritzy and St Xavier's High School, Shivaji Park and Dadar Union to understand the remarkable phenomenon of Sunil Gavaskar.

In Sunil Gavaskar's autobiography *Sunny Days* there is a paragraph devoted to St Xavier's High School. It reads:

I joined St Xavier's High School which had a fairly good cricket team at that time. While we were just juniors we would run during the lunch recess to watch the senior boys play. Feroz Patka was then the ideal of almost ever Xavierite and Vinay Chaudhari, the skipper, was equally popular. When St Xavier's won the Harris Shield during the Chaudhari's captaincy, every Xavierite went delirious with joy. We had inter-class matches which were very important, because the School's Junior Team was selected on the basis of performances in these encounters.

Even on holidays we went to play the school matches, very often with just one leg-guard and no batting gloves. I used to bowl, also, at that time and managed to bag quite a few wickets.

In an autobiography of 264 pages, this is about the only reference, or at least significant reference, that Sunil makes to our school. When it was first published I was disappointed to find that Sunil had not dwelt a bit more on our school, and surprised that he hadn't mentioned Father Fritz who was St Xavier's cricket master. But then Sunil had confessed in his preface that the autobiography was 'an attempt to put down my stray and random thoughts in some order' and it followed the autobiographical style established by other famous cricketers. Later I learnt that Sunil invited Father Fritz to watch his first Test in Bombay against England in 1973 and more recently he has spoken of the influence of Father Fritz and his cricket dictum – 'A good-length ball you block and anything else, bang.'

But what is misleading is to suggest, as Sunil does, that it was natural that he should have gone to St Xavier's and not some other school in Bombay, natural that Xavier's should have produced the man who beat Bradman's record of 29 Test centuries and whose name has become synonomous with breaking Test cricket records all round the world. Such an impression would be totally wrong. St Xavier's had never been the great cricketing school of Bombay. During my ten years at the school, we won the Harris shield only once, the victory to which Sunil refers.

St Xavier's, as its name suggests, was a Catholic school, a Jesuit school, administered by white-robed priests, whom we called Fathers assisted by the odd 'Brother', a priest who had yet to make the grade. Not all our teachers were Jesuits, or even Catholics. For some remarkable reason a good many of our teachers were females, and a good many of them were non-Catholics. We did not encounter male teachers apart from the odd priest, until we reached the age of 14. This in an all-boys school either reflected remarkable faith or remarkable obtuseness.

Our school did have Catholic students but they were, like my friend Hubert, poor Catholics whose education the school subsidised. I vividly recalled how the presence of some of these poor Catholics in my class used to goad a Parsee female teacher, a rather stern type – attractive in a curious sort of way – into demented fury. It may have been born out of sexual frustration, but her contempt for the poor Catholics she had in her class, was total. She would make their rather ill-kept clothes, their total lack of scholastic ability, their lackadaisical general demeanour a target of direct assault. She would pick on them individually asking them questions she knew they could not answer. Then she would berate them, 'You are privileged. You get free tuition here. Yet, look at the way you dress. You may be poor but can't you even spare some soap? Poor does not mean you should wear dirty clothes. You don't even make an attempt to study.'

This female teacher's views probably reflected the views of a good many of the non-Catholic teachers in our school, and many of the non-Catholic students. That she could express it so openly in a Catholic school, where her paymasters were Jesuit priests, gives some idea of the school, and the curious nature of co-existence of different communities that prevails in India. Whenever I have mentioned to my English friends that I was educated at a Jesuit school in Bombay, their reaction has been an interesting mixture of horror and bewilderment. The horror arises from the English distrust of Catholicism which still exists, the bewilderment from the realisation that in India there are Catholics. My English friends are even more surprised when I tell them that my Jesuit school made no attempt to convert me, or at least not directly. In that sense the Jesuit Fathers of St Xavier's matched the British Raj who frowned on conversion and let the Hindus and Muslims get on with their particular beliefs.

Most of the students at St Xavier's were non-Catholics – Hindus, Muslims, Parsees from the middle- and upper middle-class families of Bombay. They had been attracted to the school because, while the fees were relatively low, the standard of education was supposed to be excellent. We were, of course, open to Catholic influences. In all our class rooms, just above the blackboard, there was the figure of Christ on the cross. Four times a day, we bowed our heads before this figure, crossed ourselves and said the prayers of the Lord. Twice a day we sought blessing before class and again after lunch; twice we sought forgiveness for our sins, just before the lunch break and finally, before going home at 4.30 pm. In unison we all learned to mumble our prayers in low monotones, quickly cross ourselves and get on with more desirable pursuits. There was never any danger that this would convert us. The school did not expect it, or want it, and our parents did not fear it.

What the school did was promote a rational outlook which, in subtle ways, was subversive of traditional Indian beliefs. Thus Father Fritz would often try to convince us that it was natural that a man should choose his own wife. 'Your parents may tell you that the female is a cow and for years you will believe it, but the day will come when you will tell your parents that even if all females are cows, I would like to have a cow.' It was in such ways, and through moral science, that the school tried to influence us. Catholic boys went for catechism classes, we non-Catholics had moral science which was generalised, albeit Catholic-influenced propaganda in favour of God's existence.

Sunil has never spoken about the effect all this had on him and his cricket. But he cannot but have been marked by that special stamp that St Xavier's put on all of us. The stamp of exclusiveness that set us apart from the rest of the community we lived in. A superiority based on our supposed mastery of the English language, our sophistication and our worldy wisdom compared to our contemporaries. The very physical location of our school seemed to emphasise our superiority. It was right next door to a municipal school. Schooling is neither compulsory nor universal in India, and millions just cannot afford to go to school. Municipal schools are run in the major cities by the local municipality, the Indian equivalent of councils, and are meant for the slightly better-off among the urban poor who have a bit of money to spare after meeting their daily necessities. They send their children to these schools in the almost forlorn hope that this will improve their job prospects. The schools generally teach them the language of the state in which they are situated, provide a few years of unsatisfactory education and release them into the urban jungle.

The municipal school was just beyond our playground, and ran along one side of it. During our lunch and other recesses, it was part of our pastime to watch the students of this school. We were told they were poor and they looked poor. We were told they were hungry and they looked hungry, we were told they were ill-educated and ill-mannered, and they looked it. I cannot speak of their feelings, but from our side of the fence there was some pity and mostly relief that we were not part of that jungle. They were part of the unnamed, never mentioned enemy, those who did not speak English and were incapable of simulating our Westernised thoughts.

111

It was not merely the municipal school poor we despised. We also despised those who were evidently richer than us, and for much the same reasons: that they could not speak English. And in despising them we were expressing certain views of society. We had a term for these people: *Guju Bhais* and *Mani Bhen*, meaning Gujerati brothers and sisters. They were not all Gujeratis, the very successful business community from which Mahatma Gandhi sprang, but in our imagination any well-off person who couldn't speak English well, was quickly dubbed an undesirable Guju. We were aware of their riches, but we consoled ourselves with the fact that they had no learning. They could be seen on a Sunday evening promenading along the sea front at Marine Drive, their radios blaring forth loud music, their dress and manner struggling to be modern but failing awkwardly and their behaviour generally clownish and unsuitable. Their riches did not bother us because we believed, with some justification, that they had made their money by defrauding taxes. Perhaps there was envy here because they had clearly done well out of free, independent India which Nehru was constantly telling us, was ours to inherit. The more they flaunted their money, the more we despised them. They may have the money, we said, but they do not know how to use it. We of the middle classes may be limited in our riches, but we have the sophistication and the wit to enjoy what we have.

This, then, was Sunil Gavaskar's school inheritance. What was there that helped him to achieve his greatness? The school gave him, as it gave all of us, poise, confidence, belief in oneself and command over the English language. This last quality is not quite as trivial as it may appear. We, Sunil and I, grew up in India in the immediate post-independence years. All around us Nehru, through eloquence and personal magnetism, tried to create a new, independent India, an India which was nominally anti-English and where the English language should have been shunned. Its constitution provided for English to be replaced by Hindi as a national language by 1960. But as the English departed from India's shores, Indians seemed to be free from the invisible yoke that had prevented them from taking to the English language. Our politicians declaimed about the need to speak Hindi but sent their sons to English-speaking schools, and many found that a command of the English language was very useful in opening doors.

What else did Sunil receive from school? I think he found the belief in his cricket from Father Fritz. I have said that St Xavier's

112

was not a great cricket school and it was not. But cricket was played, incessantly, during the short mid-morning break, during the lunch recess, after school, on Thursdays, on Sundays, at every available opportunity, apart from the three months between June and September when torrential rain swept Bombay.

Father Fritz was tall, rather angular and, again by Indian standards, very fair of skin, the most significant thing about him, and one that never ceased to amaze us, was his accent. This was very clipped, and it seemed to us to be dreadfully English, peppered with phrases like 'You two-pice chaps', or 'You load of wash outs'. This heightened the exotic air which made him such a novelty. We were never sure of his origins. He looked Indian, but seemed so English in his manner that we considered him a foreigner – despite his almost touching display of Indian patriotism. In fact the greater his patriotic fervour and emphasis on being Indian, the more it seemed as if he were a foreigner who had decided to be more Indian than the Indians.

All this far from diminishing Fritz in our eyes increased his status. If anything it put him on a completely different plane from the other Jesuit Padres, as we called the Fathers – though, never to their face. We liked very little about those Padres, and, in fact, told mocking and even scurrilous tales about most of them. Never more so than when we saw one of our Padres with a nun from a neighbouring convent. We derived much malicious delight when one of our Padres turned out to be an American, who looked like a film star, was supposed to have the reputation of a rake and disappeared from our school in somewhat dubious circumstances.

Our Principal was a thin, frail, sour-looking man called Father Miranda. We were convinced that he had only one lung, largely I think due to his frailness and instantly dubbed him 'one lung kid'. There was nothing kiddish about him, if anything he was always very severe, hardly ever smiled and was not particularly approachable. He seemed to radiate a certain evil. Not all our Padres were as daunting as Miranda, but they were a very mixed bunch, many of them Spanish who spoke little English and a few of them providing a rich feast for our scurrilously imaginative tales.

Fritz was different. Patrician, aloof, moving in his own world he was far removed from what we saw as the machinations of Miranda and the curious goings on of lesser Padres. Quite early in our school career, Fritz had been dubbed Fritzy, and this

113

abbreviation denoted both affection and warmth. Fritzy, we came to believe, was capable of anything. I well remember the morning after I played in my first inter-class football match. Matches within the school, whether cricket or football, or any other sport, were very important and formed the backbone of the sporting system at St Xavier's. I cannot remember what happened in the match except that I played as a burly left-back who, failing to get the ball, often got the man. There were two other defenders in the game even burlier than me and, the next day, on the school noticeboard, Fritz pinned a report of the match. The report was fair enough though what was astonishing, and very Fritzy, was a photograph. This purported to be a photograph of the match, showing two very large players tackling for the ball, the caption identified two players as Chandra of our team and Devdas of the oppposing team. In fact the photograph was not of our inter-class match at all. Nobody took photographs of such matches. What Fritz had done was to clip a photograph of an English first division match, reprinted in *Sport and Pastime,* then India's leading sports magazine and pretend it represented our puny football match. The idea that Chandra and Devdas, then two Indian 12 year olds, could match up to two burly English first division players was comical. But we admired Fritzy's cheek in suggesting such comparisons. Later, when we quizzed him about it, he explained that his intention was to demonstrate what a real game was like and set us a standard.

For Fritzy was a great man for enunciating the broad principle. If he liked something, or somebody, he made it very clear quickly. Mostly he disliked a great many things, and a great many people, and we were always on our guard against falling foul of Fritzy. But what Fritzy brought to our lives were his convictions and his ability to motivate others. It was this that first brought Sunil Gavaskar to my notice.

I must have been 14, Sunil was probably 12. Fourteen meant we were two, three years away from the coveted matriculation and just about beginning to enjoy being a senior boy at school. One evening a group of us senior boys were talking to Father Fritz. As I recall we were standing on one of the balconies that overlooked the school ground. One end of the school playground housed garages for the school buses which ferried students to and from the school. For some reason the garage doors were invariably painted red, and when shut provided a most convenient, impromptu, wicket. Suddenly, as we leaned over the balcony, we saw a solitary little fellow in front of the red garage doors. Senior boys at school tend to be dismissive of their juniors, but even without this prejudice, Sunil looked comical. He was still wearing his school uniform of dirty beige shirt and pants, except being a junior he hadn't graduated to long trousers as we had. He even wore the recently introduced school tie. All this was supplemented by the full cricket gear. Pads, gloves, even a cap. The pads seemed to come to his chin, as he repeatedly and religiously played forward; every now and again we would catch a glimpse of the back of his shorts and his bare legs. It was too much of a temptation and we mocked and laughed with great pleasure.

I do not know whether Sunil heard Fritzy's roar of disapproval, it was certainly loud and very severe. Turning on us he said in his most clipped English accent 'You load of wash outs. You think you can play cricket. You are just two-pice chaps. You'll never be cricketers. That boy will be a great cricketer.'

We were used to Fritzy's verbal broadsides, but this one was very odd. It ran counter to everything Xavier's was meant to stand for. St Xavier's was an all-round school, which gave its pupils a good general education but did not seek to make them excellent in any one thing. Though nobody would have admitted it then, or even now, St Xavier's had a slightly dilettantish air. Its good scholastic students were good at their studies but they did not match up to the best in Bombay. In sport they put up a good fight, very rarely won and certainly did not believe in sacrificing everything for victory. In fact dedication in pursuit of any one thing was somehow an un-Xavierite trait.

However, Sunil avoided dilettantism because his dedication was real, and because Fritzy was committed to him. Fritzy had a way of conveying his commitment which was so passionate and touching that it remained with your for many years. I experienced it myself, a couple of years after the Sunil episode, when Fritzy took us for English, and with one throwaway sentence made me believe I could aspire to be a writer. It was years before I realised how much those words were to mean to me and how much they were to sustain me when writing seemed so very far away. Something of the same Fritzy commitment must have been conveyed to Sunil.

But did St Xavier's do anything else for Sunil Gavaskar and his cricket? Here I am inclined to agree with Milind Rege, Sunil's

115

contemporary, and under whose captaincy Sunil played for the school. Rege has written, 'At St Xavier's High School where Sunil studied, he was like every other cricketer. In fact there was little or no encouragement for us at Xavier's. We played cricket on a mat which was half the length of a cricket pitch. Later, we graduated to turf wickets – the turf being in the form of red mud spread evenly on a hard bumpy outfield.'

So between the half matting and the not-quite-proper turf, we played a lot of our school cricket. Its heart and soul were inter-class matches where a good performance brought the player to the notice of Father Fritz and the school selectors. I think one year an attempt at school trials to alert good cricketers was made. But there was never any attempt at coaching cricketers or bringing them up. We played a lot of cricket, but little of it was good cricket. We played for fun and those of us who had some ability went on to play for the school. Xavier's cricket had a brittle charm which can pass for substance at that age, and that seemed to be personified by Feroz Patka.

Sunil at school never had the sort of aura that came naturally to Patka, and if the truth be told it was Milind Rege who was considered the really gifted cricketer at school. For various reasons Rege, though he played for Bombay, never made it in international cricket. At school the cricket pundits were convinced that he would make his name as a cricketer and display to a wider world the leadership qualities that Xavier's sought to inculcate.

At school Sunil appeared to be good but he was not particularly exceptional. The first time he had played for the school he had batted number ten, scored thirty not out and found himself in the next day's *Times of India* as 'G. Sunil 30 not out'. It was when he moved to a higher grade of cricket, the inter-schools Gooch-Behar, then the inter-collegiate Rohinton Baria competitions that Sunil revealed what an unusually perceptive cricket journalist, Sharad Kotnis, described as a 'Bradmanesque streak'.

However, it was not only Jesuit discipline that helped to shape Sunil as a cricketer, but also his own Hindu Maharastria work ethic. Although nobody who grew up in Bombay, and knew of Shivaji Park or Dadar Union, or experienced the peculiar Maharastrian *angst*, could be unaware of it, yet, in the millions of words that have been written on Sunil, nobody has referred to it.

What is this Maharastrian angst? This Shivaji Park ingredient so crucial to the making of Sunil Gavaskar? Very simply it is wronged nationalism. Somewhat similar to the one felt in Yorkshire but infinitely more powerful. One that sees enemies everywhere and believes that the true merits and genius of Maharastrians – as the descendants of the Marhattas were called – have not been acknowledged. Shivaji Park is a symbol of that feeling. Physically Bombay is an island, or a group of seven islands joined together, representing a long, thin sausage surrounded by sea on either side. Just three main arterial roads link the commercial centre of Bombay in the south with the industrial suburban north. Shivaji Park stands in the centre of this link, and is that area's cricketing maidan: equivalent to south Bombay's Oval, Cross and Azad.

Shivaji Park is named after Shivaji the great hero of Marhatta nationalism. In the early years of the seventeenth century he raised the standard of revolt against Aurangzeb, the last great Mughal Emperor of Delhi, and so successful was he that he not only established a kingdom, but sowed the seeds of the eventual destruction of the Mughal Empire. In the struggle against the British the Maharastrians were in the forefront along with the Bengalis. When Gandhi's methods won the day the Maharastrians found they had gained little or nothing.

Bombay, the commercial capital of India, and arguably the principal city of the country, always symbolised to Maharastrians their double loss. The loss of Shivaji's Marhatta Empire that had challenged the Moghuls and resisted the British, and the loss of the pre-Gandhian political leadership. Though Shivaji, and his descendants, had never controlled Bombay – it had been a Portuguese and then a British enclave – in the Bombay of my youth the Maharastrian desire to control Bombay was evident. Try as they might, they could not achieve this. They formed the most significant proportion of the population – 42 per cent – but not the majority. They were the drawers of water and the hewers of wood. The real power in Bombay lay with the others: Parsees, efficient middle men, who had helped create commercial Bombay and, as Gandhi swept the Indian political board, his community, the Gujeratis. By the mid-1950s Gujeratis were being challenged by the Sindhis. The Bombay legend was that Sindhis, refugees from Sind which had gone to Pakistan at the time of the Indian partition, had arrived in Bombay wearing just one shirt and ended up selling shirts to everybody in the city.

What galled the Maharastrians was the fact that they were

lumped together with their hateful enemies, the Gujeratis in one composite state of Bombay, whose capital was the city of Bombay. While the rest of India was divided up into linguistic states the central government in Delhi argued that Maharastrians and Gujeratis must live together and Bombay was too important, too 'cosmopolitan' to belong only to Maharastrians. Eventually, through Gandhian-style mass action, and a certain amount of violence, the Maharastrians won their argument. A separate Maharastrian state was created with Bombay as its capital. This did nothing to change the commercial power in the city, and even today Bombay remains a city where the capital is in Gujerati and Sindhi hands – the bosses for whom the Maharastrians work.

Nowhere is the sense of injustice stronger than in the congested Maharastrian middle class of Shivaji Park. Perhaps in time some researcher will tell us about the mainspring which motivates the Maharastrian middle classes of Shivaji Park. It is already easy to discern the broad outline. The intense desire to succeed, the need to prove to the rest of cosmopolitan Bombay and India that they are a force and a certain feeling, which they share with the Bengalis, that they have been wronged by the rest of India, ruled – or ruined – by Gujeratis and upstart Sindhis. The Maharastrian middle class nurses a deep sense of wronged justice and that can always be a very powerful force, be it in politics or sport.

How much or little Sunil actually shares these Maharastrian Shivaji Park middle-class ambitions is not known, but he is fully aware of them and must have been influenced by them. Like any good Maharastrian, Sunil learnt the Marhatta history early, from his mother and father – and at the age of 10 there was Vasu Paranjape and Dadar Union, which plays its cricket on a maidan about a mile or so from Shivaji Park. It was Vasu who gave Sunil his nickname Sunny, a name whose endless permutations along the lines of Sunny Days, Sunny Plays, Sunny Records – and even more ridiculous ones – are a delight to Indian sub-editors. If Sunil had a mentor in cricket then it was undoubtedly Paranjape. Today he works in the same Bombay firm as Sunil and continues to act as a sort of father confessor.

In December 1983 Sunil returned to Bombay after a quite traumatic Test match against the West Indians in Calcutta. Sunil had equalled Bradman's record of twenty-nine Test centuries in the Delhi test a few weeks previous to this and an expectant, characteristically tumultuous Bengali crowd were waiting in

118

feverish expectation to see Sunil actually break the record. But he was out to the first ball of the match, to Marshall. He lasted a little longer in the second innings, but he got out with a reckless, very un-Sunil like stroke. The Indians, who at one stage had looked like winning the match, collapsed ignominiously and almost every-body in India seemed to hold Gavaskar personally responsible for the Indian defeat. Forgotten was his Delhi performance, and Indians, who can veer alarmingly from praise to abuse, showered choice epithets on him. One cricket supporter sent him a photograph of a chappal (slipper) with an arrow pointing to the picture and the inscription, 'I present this with due apologies for your performance against the West Indies'. In the Indian tradition the Order of the Chappal is damning. It is quite common for political demonstrators to indicate their disgust by hurling chappals at their political enemies. How rattled Sunil was by all this, I do not know, but he promised Paranjape that he would make amends. The result was his scoring his thirtieth century at the Madras Test and breaking Bradman's record.

Paranjape tells the story with no great dramatic flourish, almost a if it was inevitable. But then to Paranjape it undoubtedly was. He had done much to instil this Marhatta determination in Sunil. This is how Paranjape would later recall Sunil's introduction to Bombay club cricket:

> I remember Sunny as a youngster of ten plus, coming along with his father to watch Dadar Union play on Sundays. Eagerly pressing for a knock before the start of the matches, I distinctly recall the obvious and conspicuous straightness of his bat. Even the seriousness during those knocks used to be beyond his years.

We can picture the Dadar Union scene. The tin, asbestos shed, that has clearly seen better days – next to it, a few shacks for the malis and their children, who can just be glimpsed playing in the mud in front of the shed. Behind the shed, half obscured, a block of flats with its mixture of grime and dust and Indian domesticity. And just in front of the shed, instead of a pitch fit for a conquering hero, there is a mound of weeds that would shame any weekend gardener.

Yet in Gavaskar's recall of his crucial Dadar Union days, there is no mention of such disabilities. Partly this is the Indian ability, necessary for survival, to ignore the squalor and poverty that surrounds almost every public place. It is this that enables rich Indians to ignore the beggars outside the restaurants and walk blithely in and enjoy a sumptuous meal. For Sunil the Dadar Union's sumptuousness was provided by Vasu Paranjape, the Captain of the team, and Vithal 'Marshall' Patil, good Maharastrians and forceful personalities. Paranjape impressed on Sunil his outlook on the game, which was 'a blend of the carefree approach of the West Indians and the bulldog tenacity of the Australians . . . as a fielder he was magnificent and his aggressive batting won many a hopeless match for Dadar Union. His captaincy was as dynamic as his batting, and he loved a challenge.' Patil, or Marshall as he was called in the Indian tradition of giving English nicknames to their compatriots, was the Dadar Union coach. He lived and breathed cricket and encouraged Sunil by not only bowling to him at every possible opportunity – a distinct advantage as he could swing the ball – but also by providing him with a mental stimulus. 'Often', Sunil would later recall, 'he would drop in at our house later after dinner and say "Sunny, a century tomorrow". I think he had more confidence in my cricketing ability than I had myself.'

Paranjape's influence was so pervasive that most Shivaji Park Maharastrians, interested in cricket, seem to have fallen under his spell. I remember talking about Paranjape with a staunch Maharastrian nationalist, who worked in my father's firm, and was struck by the emotion that Paranjape generated even in such a grown man. In those years, Paranape's Dadar Union and Shivaji Park as such had a cricketing mission similar to the one that inspired Maharastrian politicians. Right from the inception of the Ranji trophy in 1934, the state of Bombay had been represented by a cricket team. However, during the days of the Raj, the state of Bombay was huge and in addition to the Bombay team, parts of the state were also allowed to enter the Ranji trophy. So Gujerat had a team as did Maharastra. The Gujerat team was centred around Ahmedabad, the Maharastra team around Poona, now called Pune and the actual Bombay state team around the capital city of Bombay. It was as if Yorkshire had been allowed to enter three teams, one centred around Leeds, another around Bradford and a third, possibly around Harrogate or Scarborough.

When the Maharastrian politicians won their argument, the old Bombay state was divided between Gujerat, with its capital at Ahmedabad, and Maharastra with its capital at Bombay. The Ranji

120

trophy continued to have three teams: Bombay, Maharastra and Gujerat. But for the Maharastrians living and playing their cricket in Bombay, this produced a curious situation. There were now two Maharastrian teams, the original Maharastrian side centred around Poona, and the Old Bombay state side, but now exclusively devoted to Bombay city. Bombay's cricket team reflected the cosmopolitan nature of Bombay society. The great Bombay cricketer and Captain was Polly Umrigar, Faroukh Engineer, another Parsee, kept wicket and one of Bombay's leading players was Gulbhai Ramchand, a Sindhi. Maharastrians formed part of the team, but did not run it or control it.

The tension between Maharastrians and non-Maharastrians was reflected in the struggle between the Bombay cricket association, which was Maharastrian dominated, and which resented the pre-eminence of the Cricket Club of India, at that time India's MCC. The CCI was more cosmopolitan; owned Brabourne stadium, Bombay's test centre, and every Test match saw a running battle between the Bombay Cricket Association and the CCI about allocation of Test match tickets. Eventually so bitter was the struggle that Bombay Cricket Association decided to take cricket away from the CCI and Wankhede stadium was built a mere quarter of a mile away. By the time the first Test was played there in 1974 the Maharastrians had asserted their control over the Bombay cricket team. But in the decade preceding that, as Sunil grew into cricketing maturity, the battle for the control of Bombay cricket was yet to be decided.

Sunil has never spoken or written about this. Possibly he would profess total indifference to all this Maharastrian feeling. When recently, a *Sunday Times* writer, Dudley Doust, went to India to write a profile on Sunil Gavaskar I suggested to him that he might look into Sunil's Maharastrian, Shivaji Park background. But when Dudley asked Sunil about this he dismissed it. No, he didn't feel particularly Maharastrian, he was an Indian. Why, his wife Marshniel was not a Maharastrian but a girl from UP, a province in northern India and he frankly did not bother much about her origins. To Dudley this answer seemed conclusive enough. In fact, though, it is very much the answer I would have expected a good Xavierite to give. After all we were taught at school. 'You are Indian first, then anything else. When they ask you who you are, do not say you are a Bengali, or a Maharastrian, or any other regional variation. Say you are Indian.'

Perhaps some clue to Sunil's real feelings on the subject can be found in *Idols*, which published in 1984 contains Sunil's reflections on thirty-one circketers. Nearly all the well-known cricketers of the last two decades are there and most of the names would be easily recognised by any cricket follower. However, the style of the essays is fulsome praise rather than appraisal. Only one cricketing essay stands out – the one on Padmakar Shivalkar. He is also only one of two in this list who never played Test cricket or even came near to it. He is hardly known outside his native Bombay. It is precisely because of Gavaskar's ability to portray Shivalkar's predicaments and problems, a left-arm spinner hoping to play for India at a time when Bishan Singh Bedi was at his height, that makes the essay stand out from the rest. Gavaskar neatly highlights Shivalkar's Shivaji Park background, the character and humour that gave rise to his nickname Paddy, and the cheerfulness and determination with which he nurtured his skill as a left-arm spinner, knowing full well that he would never play for his country.

Gavaskar is able to do it because he has known Shivalkar since his teens, and clearly shares the widespread Bombay feeling of the late 1960s and early 1970s that Shivalkar was unlucky. Shivalkar's story seemed to symbolise the Maharastrian angst. In this essay Gavaskar seems to be paying homage to the cricketing memory of a man, lost to possible international greatness because of rotten luck and perhaps, prejudiced authorities.

There are some in India who would see Sunil's Maharastrian background as a clue to his curious love/hate relationship with the Indian public. Indians respect Sunil but they also fear him. He is not, for instance, able to invoke the sort of warmth that is awarded to Kapil Dev, or even to his own brother-in-law, Viswanath, probably the most loved of all Indian cricketers.

Part of the Indian diffidence may be that for all his records and his achievements, Gavaskar's domestic record has always lagged behind his Test record. By the end of the 1975–6 season, page 123 shows how his Test record compared with his record in the Ranji trophy, the major Indian domestic competition.

This is quite extraordinary. Comparable figures for Boycott and Bradman would show phenomenal run-scoring in domestic cricket far outstripping that of international cricket. Partly this may be due to the growth of international cricket, but more perhaps because Sunil is not an accumulator. Only twice in domestic

Test

Versus	Year	M	I	N.O.	H.S.	Runs	Average	100s	Bowling Runs	W	Fielding Average	Caught
West Indies	1970/1	4	8	3	220	774	154.80	4	9	0	–	1
England	1971	3	6	0	57	144	24.00	–	42	0	–	5
England	1972/3	5	10	1	69	224	23.88	–	7	0	–	2
England	1974	3	6	0	101	217	36.16	1	5	0	–	1
West Indies	1974/5	2	4	0	86	108	27.00	–	–	–	–	1
New Zealand	1975/6	3	5	1	116	266	66.50	1	–	–	–	5
West Indies	1975/6	4	7	0	156	390	57.14	2	–	–	–	2
TOTAL		24	46	5	220	2123	51.77	8	63	0	–	17

Ranji Trophy

Versus	Year	M	I	N.O.	H.S.	Runs	Average	100s	Bowling Runs	W	Fielding Average	Caught
	1969/70	2	3	1	114	141	70.51	1	–	–	–	6
	1970/1	2	3	0	176	307	102.33	2	19	1	19.00	0
	1971/2	3	5	0	282	494	98.80	2	21	0	–	8
	1972/3	7	12	2	160	579	57.90	3	0	1	6.00	16
	1973/4	6	9	1	84	248	31.00	–	–	–	–	11
	1974/5	5	6	2	96	203	50.75	–	6	0	–	4
	1975/6	4	5	1	190	510	127.50	3	4	0	–	5
TOTAL		29	43	7	282	2483	68.97	11	50	2	25.00	50

cricket has he accumulated more than 500 runs – a benchmark in India – a season.

But even that can hardly explain the anti-Gavaskar venom that is spewed out by the Indian press. At the end of the 1984–5 season against England, a dismal one for India, there was much press coverage on India's one great hero of the series: Mohammed Azharuddin. India's leading weekly *Sunday* published a cover story about him. Within that cover story was this article about Sunil Gavaskar. An article that deserves to be quoted in full, just to indicate the emotions that Sunil can arouse.

IS GAVASKAR JEALOUS OF AZHARUDDIN?

For over a decade Sunil Gavaskar was Indian cricket. He was the best opening batsman in the world, one of the greatest Indian batsmen ever, an astute and successful captain, and the holder of just about every batting record in test cricket. In the hit-and-miss world of Indian cricket, he was a phenomenon. With success came fame, fat paychecks and the adulation and affection of millions, something which Gavaskar may well have taken for granted.

More recently, however, there have been more ruins than runs for Gavaskar, a phase which has coincided with the rise of Mohammed Azharuddin. His first series has been as magnificent as Gavaskar's 1971 tour of the West Indies and he has quickly replaced his captain as the cult figure of the game. Cricket-lovers all over the country are already lining up behind Azhar. Is Gavaskar missing his status as a Messiah? And more importantly, has he deliberately tried to place obstacles in the young super-star's way?

With Sandeep Patil dropped after his suicidal dismissal in the lost Delhi test, one place in the middle order was vacant. It was Gavaskar's plan to drop down the order, not to give it a semblance of stability as was the original excuse, but to find his touch – his failures with the bat were continuing. But the selectors, the men Gavaskar had once called jokers, strongly, and this time rightly opposed his plan. This was the right time, they decided, to blood a promising young cricketer and Gavaskar would have to open the innings. And in what was one of the dreariest test matches in recent history, only Azharuddin sparkled.

Again, after Gavaskar's by-now-all-too-familiar early dismissal in the Indian first innings at Kanpur, it was surprisingly Azharuddin who replaced his skipper at the batting crease. Admittedly, Azhar was the man in form and Gavaskar's Bombay colleague Dilip Vengsarkar the regular one-drop batsman in the side was not, but it was only Azhar's fourth test innings and there was another far more experienced batsman. Mohinder Amarnath who has regularly batted in this pivotal number three position. And why was a young batsman pushed up the batting order just to protect an out-of-form senior batsman?

When Azharuddin did get his third and by far his best century on the second morning, his teammates applauded from the players' enclosure as the crowds rose to a man to greet their new hero. Only the man who ought to have led the applause was very conspicuously absent. Since Sivaramakrishnan had sent the English side spinning to their doom during those brief moments of euphoria at Bombay few things had gone right for India, and this was one of the few. The Gavaskar of old, more a leader of a combative, fighting-fit team, than of a surly bunch of highly-talented individuals would have been the first on the balcony. This time he refused to make an appearance. What kept Gavaskar away during Azhar's and India's moment of glory may never be revealed. Was it pique that a man far younger and far more inexperienced had stolen his thunder? Or was he simply scared of showing his face in the enclosure and facing a crowd which has adopted Gavaskar-baiting as a bloodsport?

Then, with the wicket proving to be a traditional Kanpur sleeping beauty which even Sivaramakrishnan, the prince charming of Indian spinners could not awaken, did Gavaskar honestly expect to dismiss a side which had batted for over two days and scored over 400 runs in just over two hours? Or was it just another gesture of empty defiance, crafty enough to prevent Azhar, batting on a brilliantly improvised 54 from getting another hundred and re-writing the cricket books all over again? Gavaskar himself had admitted that God was an Englishman and so, could not have hoped for divine assistance. In any case, getting a test team out in 80 minutes and 20 mandatory overs on a batsman's paradise would have required not only extraordinary slices of luck, but a course in black magic as well.

Is Gavaskar envious of Azharuddin? Is he trying to prevent Azhar from reaching the pinnacle of glory he himself had reached? Perhaps, the limited overs matches in Australia next month will provide the answer.

It is difficult to imagine a similar article appearing in the English press. But while the Indian writer reflects the bitterness that Gavaskar arouses, has Sunil, perhaps, contributed to it? There is the celebrated feud with Kapil Dev, the fact that he has not been able to project an all-India image, his quest for money and, now, a certain loss of concentration. I am inclined to agree with Pataudi that there is a perverse streak in Gavaskar that may have been worsened by the pressure-cooker atmosphere that Indians inflict on their celebrities. While the charity and obvious generosity of Indians can be quite marvellous, it can also be overwhelming and the family focus of Indian life make – at least in the urban sphere – cool-headed contemplation difficult. But perhaps, Gavaskar's career and his relationship with the Indian public prove that singleminded dedication has its pitfalls. He's certainly a hero and a great cricketer but one the public finds difficult to live with.

CHAPTER 7

The Nawabi Legend

In December 1980, just after India had beaten Pakistan in the third Test match in Bombay, the following graffiti appeared on the walls of certain parts of the city. It read:

INDIA PLAYS WITH THIRTEEN PEOPLE –
ELEVEN PLAYERS AND TWO UMPIRES.

Indians have a much more relaxed attitude towards their own umpires than most non-Indians give them credit for. That graffiti was still on the walls of Bombay when I visited India almost a year later. Then, too, umpiring decisions were threatening to bedevil a Test series. The first Test between India and England was being played in Bombay, and Keith Fletcher and his men were convinced it had already been lost because of Indian umpiring decisions. I remember talking to a few of my Indian friends, the day before England lost the match and one of them was supremely confident that India would win. 'You just watch; there will be three lbw decisions – Boycott, Fletcher and Botham.' Fletcher and Boycott were indeed given out lbw, but to play back on a crumbling fourth day wicket suggested an optimism that would have been misplaced even in front of English umpires. Botham, more characteristically, was out trying to hit the ball into the Arabian sea.

But the graffiti that had appeared on the Bombay streets was no self-deprecatory Indian joke. It appeared mostly in the Muslim areas of Bombay – clearly the work of Indian Muslims expressing an unequivocal opinion on that controversial Test. The whiff of controversy is evident even from the scrupulously objective reports in Wisden. The pitch, it said, presented problems from the first day, so much so that Gavaskar, the Indian Captain, who had decided to bat on winning the toss, was out for four by a ball that stopped. The Indians secured their initial advantage because they won the toss but the anger that prompted the graffiti was caused by the number of lbw decisions given by the umpires against the visiting Pakistanis. Four of them were out lbw in the second innings, as against only Viswanath in the Indian second innings. Wisden, describing Miandad's lbw said 'considering that the ball was turning so readily, he might have been unfortunate to be given out'.

To the Indian Muslims Miandad's dismissal was not chance but part of a conspiracy. They reflected the charges made by the Pakistani cricketers who not only alleged bias on the part of the umpires, but also claimed that the ground authorities in Bombay had doctored the pitch after the match had started. For Indians, naturally suspicious of Pakistan and her actions, the fact that Indian Muslims' views agreed with those of the Pakistani cricket team raised all the old doubts. By the time I visited Bombay the Test, indeed the entire series, which the Indians won 2–0, had reopened many of the arguments I had personally experienced almost twenty years ago. Then the debate had taken place behind closed doors. Now it was the subject of cover stories. Very simply it was: when India played Pakistan, what was the position of the large minority Indian Muslims? Did they support India, Pakistan or remain neutral?

We are dealing with what one of India's greatest writers Nirad C. Chaudhuri calls 'the least of the minorities' in India. I am inclined to say we are dealing with the Indian nigger. I shall explain both terms in greater detail but first an account of the historical background is necessary.

Of India's population of over seven hundred million, some seventy seven million are Muslims. The great majority of these are descendants of converts to Islam from lower-caste Hindu society. A small minority among them could, possibly, claim descent from the Muslim conquerors who arrived in India in a wave of invasions that started in the eleventh century. The Muslim conquest of India was a gradual, long drawn out process which started in Sind in the eighth century, and ended with the Mughal rule in Delhi between the fifteenth and the eighteenth centuries. The Muslims never conquered the whole of India, or even ruled over all of it, not even at the height of the Mughal Empire. As D. P. Singhal, in his recently published *A History of the Indian People*, puts it while the Turki-Afghan invaders were mainly interested in loot and plunder – destroying innumerable Hindu temples and icons, carrying off immense wealth and appropriating businesses – the later Muslim rulers were woven into the India pattern 'drawn by the tolerance and responsiveness of the Indian mind and their own capacity for absorption and imitation. Throughout India, an initial clash was followed by fusion and synthesis.'

The popular conception however was different. The Hindu recollection of the Muslim invasion of India was that of the classical conqueror and plunderer. The Muslim Muhammed of Ghazni is seen swooping down from the lush inviting mountains of the Hindu Kush to repeatedly invade India, destroy the wonderfully rich temple of Somnath and the perfection and beauty of the pre-Islamic Hindu Raj. In this Hindu version, highly selective and somewhat biased, the Hindu fall dates from Muhammed of Ghazni's repeated invasions of India. It symbolises the archetypal Muslim interloper, the man who covets Hindu wealth and rapes Hindu women. To many Hindus the Muslim is ignorant, uncouth, dirty, often has a short, funny beard and a very peculiar un-Indian (read un-Hindu) cap. What is more he does not wear the *dhoti* as most Hindus do, but a *lungi.* To most Westerners the difference between a dhoti and a lungi may seem academic. Both are long pieces of cloth, worn by men, and wrapped round the body from the waist downwards. But in Hindu eyes the dhoti is elegant, invariably white, and draped round the body with a certain delicacy. The lungi is generally of bizarre, multi-colour material and wrapped round the body, rather more casually, like a towel.

Muslim preference for the lungi could be explained in terms of economics, the lungi being cheaper, but uncharitable Hindus give a different explanation. This is that the Muslim, or at least the ghetto Muslims, preferred the lungi because they can discard it easily to indulge in their favourite activity: sex. Muslims, like Jews, are circumcised. And in India they are referred to, rather crudely, as *katela,* meaning the cut one. Sexual potency may or may not be increased by circumcision, but it is widely believed in India that this is one of the forces that drives the ghetto Muslim and his sexual potency is only equalled by his lust for Hindu women.

It was our driver, Shankar, who first told me about katelas. One evening in 1946 when the Hindu-Muslim riots had gripped Bombay, Shankar, minding his own business, was travelling home. But his home was in Mazgoan, and he had to pass through certain Muslim ghettos to get there. He was stopped by a Muslim mob and asked 'Who are you? What is your name?' He was petrified. To have given his real name would have been to commit suicide. As he stood undecided, the mob edged closer, threatening to take off his trousers and reveal his true identity. Suddenly Shankar realised that in his pocket he had the means of possible salvation: a cross. He took it out, and pretended to be a Christian. He claimed his name was Stanley. The Muslims were convinced and he escaped.

However alongside this general fear and suspicion in personal situations Hindus and Muslims would often get on very well. My father employed Muslim workers, traded with Muslims and, indeed, his favourite business contact was a Muslim who became a good family friend.

Of course not all Muslims lived in ghettos, there were educated, cultured Muslims too and, as India is a secular state, there were Muslims occupying high political positions. In the years since Indian independence, India has had two Muslim presidents, a Muslim chief of defence staff, several Muslim judges, a couple of chief justices of the Indian Supreme Court, a great number of Muslim politicians and ministers in central and state politics and several senior Muslim civil servants. Also for ten years, a Muslim was India's cricket Captain. The Nawab of Pataudi, popularly known as Tiger.

Nirad Chaudhuri has suggested that this was the result of the Hindu-Muslim political collaboration between 1917 and 1922 when the two communities successfully came together to fight the British, and the personality of Nehru, who was 'by social and cultural affiliations' more of a Muslim then a Hindu, in so far as he was 'anything Indian at all'. Nehru, according to Chaudhuri, came from a family which was open to Islamic influences and found Muslims more sophisticated than Hindus. Nehru's personality may well have provided Muslims with a certain position in India after independence, but the case of the Nawab of Pataudi and the role he played in cricket suggests that the broader topic of Muslim participation in Indian cricket is somewhat more complicated than that.

This extract from a double-page spread in the magazine *Sports World*, entitled 'Face to Face with a Tiger' gives one a feeling of the position Pataudi occupies in modern Indian cricket.

If you've got a minute, try this experiment. Take a ball, close one eye, toss it up and try catching it. The chances are you will miss. Because with one eye, you will have what is known as a 'parallax' problem. Now imagine facing Jeff Thomson, John Snow, Fred Trueman, or even Lance Gibbs with one eye. Or imagine taking a hot, low catch. And imagine doing all that with style, power, and international class. Hard to imagine an ordinary human being doing that. But what about a Tiger? Or Mansur Ali Khan – the Nawab of Pataudi? Ah! Now that's possible isn't it!

Within the first two minutes of meeting him, you'll know tiger's no pussy cat. He stalks into his lair, a brown, dark den loaded with books and a few photographs and fixes you with a steady, unblinking gaze. His agile mind ripples with tough opinions and he expresses them with the tigerish conviction. Mansur Ali Khan is every inch his epithet – Tiger.

As it happens Tiger edits *Sports World* and you may think this is just a personal plug. In fact it is an advertisement feature by Air India, using Tiger to promote the airline. What is so astonishing is not so much the overblown rhetoric which is fairly common in India, but the fact that Tiger last played cricket for India in 1974 – ten years before Air India decided to use him as their advertising symbol. Few ex-cricketers, Indian or foreign, have lasted so well. Everybody in Indian cricket knows him as Tiger, he requires no other name. When interviewed, his expert, often pithy, comments are eagerly awaited; stories of his eccentric behaviour are endlessly retold and his very presence on the cricket ground, albeit in the commentary box, is still guaranteed to create a stir.

When Tiger arrived on the scene Indian cricket desperately needed a hero. In 1958–9 the West Indies, building the first of their awesome pace attacks, had come to India and won 3–0. In 1959 India went to England and lost 5–0. In 1960–1 Pakistan came to India and all five Tests were drawn. Apart from lowly New Zealand, India, it seemed, could beat nobody. Against such a background Tiger's exploits at Winchester, Oxford and Sussex seemed like manna from heaven – another Ranji and what is more one who would play for India.

Then came the tragic accident. When everybody was predicting the greatest of futures for Pataudi – as a batsman who might rival the other great Indians who had played in England, Ranji, Duleep and his own father, the Nawab of Pataudi Senior – he was involved in a car crash and lost an eye. Sudden tragedy is by no means an Indian phenomenon, but in Indian life it seems to play a big part.

131

Almost every family tale has some tragic loss to relate. In Pataudi's case the loss was ameliorated by his ability to quickly resume cricket. Within six months of the car crash, he was making his Test debut for India, playing a swashbuckling innings, including a century in his second Test. His very first Test, the fourth in the series against Ted Dexter's England team, produced an Indian victory. Pataudi himself scored a century in the last Test and India confirmed her superiority by completing a 2–0 series victory. This is one part of the Pataudi legend. Despite his appalling handicap, he was a fine player and while Indians continuously sigh about what might have been had the car crash not taken place, they applaud the courage and skill of a player who overcame such a handicap.

Interestingly, Pataudi's great international innings always seemed to be played amidst tragedy. His memorable 148 at Leeds was played while two of his colleagues Surti and Bedi nursed injuries and could take little or no part in the match. His eighty-six at Melbourne, a year later, was played on one leg – he had a torn thigh muscle – while the rest of the Indian batsmen collapsed all around him. In both cases India lost fairly comprehensively and there were question marks about Pataudi's captaincy. The Indian batting collapse at Melbourne was due partly to Pataudi's decision to bat first on a lively, greenish wicket. But such criticisms were muted because of Tiger's batting exploits. Indian cricketing history is full of stories of the lone batsman, battling against the enemy while all his colleagues collapse round him in a heap. For example when India was defeated 4–0 at the hands of Bradman's Australians in 1947–8, Indian cricket drew some comfort from Vijay Hazare scoring a century in each innings of the Adelaide Test. On the equally disastrous 1952 tour of England, Vinoo Mankad's exploits at Lord's: 68 and 184 and five wickets led one London paper to describe the match as 'Mankad versus England'. This headline and Mankad's feats have been endlessly retold in India as if by doing so Indians could forget the damage the Australians and English had inflicted on their cricket team.

But Tiger brought to this familiar 'boy on the burning bridge' syndrome a dash, charm and style all of his own. Even his debut as India's Captain had this same feel about it. He became Captain in only his fifth Test match, at the age of 21, the youngest man to captain his country. Soon after India's 2–0 victory over England, in the spring of 1962, the Indians flew to the West Indies for a five-Test series. The Indian Captain was the left-handed opening batsman Nari Contractor. Though a dour bat, he had led India to her first serious victory over England and seemed destined to captain India for a very long time. Pataudi was appointed Vice-Captain, a decision much applauded in the country where it was seen as providing useful experience for the youngster. Nobody expected Pataudi to become Captain – at least not for some time.

India lost the first two Tests to Frank Worrell's immensely strong West Indian side, and then moved to Barbados to play the island side which, in those days, was almost as strong as a Test team. Here the second tragedy, which was to shape Pataudi's cricketing life, struck. Contractor, opening the innings as usual, ducked into a ball from Griffiths, which did not rise as expected and was led away from the field bleeding, and India was left without a captain. Pataudi as Vice-Captain took over in the third Test but could do little to prevent the Indians being thrashed 5–0.

It was another eighteen months before India played a Test series again, in 1963–4 against Mike Smith's England team. Pataudi was appointed Captain and remained so until the spring of 1971 when, in a sensational coup, he was replaced on the Chairman of the Selectors' casting vote in favour of Ajit Wadekar. Three years later, Wadekar returned from England his team beaten 3–0, he personally disgraced. Pataudi was recalled to the captaincy against Clive Lloyd's West Indians. If the first phase of his cricket captaincy was marked by defiant batting exploits, this his last series as Captain and player was marked by undistinguished batting performances but redeemed by his skills as a Captain. India lost the first two Tests and then won the next two producing a cliff-hanging final which the West Indians eventually won.

As far as the Pataudi legend is concerned it would have been totally out of character if India had actually won that final Test. The Pataudi legend was founded on dramatic losses and might-have-beens. Yet Pataudi is still considered, as the Air India advertisement put it 'one of the finest Captains India has ever had'. Pataudi himself has never had any illusions about his captaincy saying 'India has never had a good captain. In the land of the blind, a man with one eye is King!' Certainly by any international standards, Pataudi's record as Captain can hardly be described as glorious. This is his captaincy record:

133

Season	Venue	Opponent	Result
1962	West Indies	West Indies	India lost 5–0, Pataudi Captain for the last three Tests
1963–4	India	England	All five Tests drawn
1964–5	India	Australia	1–1
1964–5	India	New Zealand	India won 1–0
1966–7	India	West Indies	India lost 2–0
1967	England	England	England 3–0 (series consisted of three Tests)
1967–8	Australia	Australia	India lost 4–0 (series consisted of four Tests)
1967–8	New Zealand	New Zealand	India won 3–1. (series consisted of four Tests)
1969–70	India	New Zealand	India draw 1–1 (series consisted of four Tests)
1969–70	India	Australia	India lost 3–1 (series consisted of five Tests)
1974–5	India	West Indies	India lost 3–2

Pataudi's numerous supporters say that Tiger was unlucky. By rights he should have reaped the glory that went to Ajit Wadekar when, between 1971 and 1973, India beat West Indies in the West Indies and England in England. These victories when the spin quartet of Bedi, Prasanna, Chandrasekhar and Venkat, was at its height, provide the most glorious Test period in Indian cricket history. Tiger, so the argument goes had prepared the team that Wadekar took to glory. With better catching, India might have won the series against Australia at home in 1969–70 3–1 instead of losing it by that margin, and Wadekar was, undoubtedly, lucky to be the right man at the right place.

Perhaps so, might-have-beens are always fascinating in India, and something Indians love to indulge in. Yet contrast Wadekar's record with Pataudi's:

Season	Venue	Opponent	Result
1971	West Indies	West Indies	India won: 1–0
1971	England	England	India won: 1–0 (series consisted of three Tests)
1972–3	India	England	India won: 2–1
1974	England	England	India lost: 3–0 (series consisted of three Tests)

This is, by far, the best Test record of any Indian cricket captain. The 3–0 defeat in England was a bad one, involving a most humiliating forty-two all out by India in the second innings of the Lord's Test, but even so it seems that the punishment Wadekar received was excessive. He lost the captaincy and was virtually made to retire from Test cricket. Pataudi was recalled as Captain and was welcomed back by the Indian cricketing public as a prodigal son. At least one cricket writer felt that it was generous of Tiger to forgive the Indian Cricket Board for sacking him in such a dastardly fashion in 1971. Few recall Wadekar's captaincy with any warmth and he certainly does not have the status that Tiger enjoys. Despite Pataudi's record, almost because of it, his captaincy reign is seen as a long, lost golden age.

I well recall a conversation I had with an Indian journalist during the 1974 tour. The journalist made no bones about his anti-Wadekar views, and, confidently predicted that the Indians would have a terrible summer. When I demurred and pointed to Wadekar's record, he said that India's victory over England in 1972–3 owed much to Tiger's recall as a batsman. (Pataudi had missed the 1971 tours of West Indies and England by trying and failing to become a politician. In the low scoring 1972–3 series, his batting had been quite crucial.) My journalist friend then told me, with malicious delight, how the Indian Board had tried hard to persuade Tiger to come to England in 1974. But, according to this journalist the 'wise Tiger' had sensed that the tour would be disastrous and declined.

Now this may be apocryphal and is not dissimilar to stories seeking to explain Boycott's absence from Tests in the mid-1970s. What is revealing is that while Boycott's absence from Tests reinforced the image of the lonely recluse only willing to play on his own terms, Pataudi's absence from Tests only served to heighten the impression of a man of destiny wrongly cheated of his inheritance.

It is this that made Pataudi's captaincy seem so magical in India. During the 1963–4 series against England, his first as a proper Captain of India, the first four Tests ended in a fairly pedestrian draw. At the fifth Test, played on a perfect batting wicket in Kanpur, Pataudi won the toss. To the amazement of everybody he decided to put England in. There was nothing, conceivably, in the wicket or the atmosphere to justify his decision. England made a big score, well over 500, and the Indians, who went in to bat after two days in the field, promptly collapsed. Defeat seemed near but thanks to a century by Nadkarni, India saved the Test. When asked

135

for an explanation for his extraordinary decision, Pataudi remarked that since the first four Tests had ended in draws, he thought it was time to do something to provide the long-suffering crowd with some thrills. Although the only thrill in that Test was that of India escaping from defeat, such was Tiger's aura, that there were few recriminations about a decision which had opened up the possibility of defeat in the first place. Indeed he won applause for his marvellously eccentric thinking.

It was, perhaps, this unpredictability in Pataudi, something totally foreign to most Indians, that made him so charming and exciting. As I have said Pataudi came to the helm of affairs after two decades of captaincy that had produced draws at home and ignominious defeats abroad. Any challenge was preferable and Pataudi's captaincy walked a tantalising tightrope. He always seemed to be at the point of resigning the captaincy and, always being persuaded by the Indian cricket authorities to stay on. Just before the Indian team left for Australia on their 1967–8 tour, Pataudi actually resigned from the captaincy. The Indians had returned from England, the previous summer, beaten 3–0 in the Tests and the manager had made critical references to Pataudi's captaincy. But this was not well known and the resignation, on the eve that a crucial Duleep trophy final between the West Zone and the South Zone was to start at the Brabourne stadium, came as a shock. It overshadowed all news and I and my friends, watching the match felt a deep sense of sadness that he was going. Even Indian journalists who had been critical of his captaincy wondered who could replace him and hoped that he would think again. Throughout the match a remarkable pro-Pataudi sentiment built up and this was crowned by Pataudi, himself, scoring a double century for South Zone which enabled them to take the first innings lead against West Zone and win the Duleep trophy. By the end of the match there was no doubt that Pataudi would remain India's Captain.

Probably Pataudi's resignation stunt was meant to bring the normally faction-ridden Indian Cricket Board into line. Indian cricket, as Pataudi says, produces cricketers 'in spite of the system – not because of it'. The Indian Cricket Board is perpetually divided into factions: East versus West, North versus South, South combining with the West to down North, and throughout Pataudi's captaincy there was the chance of Chandu Borde becoming Captain. Had the Contractor accident not taken place in the West

Indies in 1962, and catapaulted Pataudi to the captaincy, Borde might well have been the Captain. He was already well established in the Indian team when Pataudi made his debut and was a reasonable Captain of Maharashtra. But Borde was condemned to be Pataudi's Vice-Captain. Preliminaries to every cricket season saw familiar speculation about Pataudi being replaced by Borde only for Pataudi to be eventually reconfirmed as Captain.

Raju Bharatan in *Indian Cricket – The Vital Phase* has provided a certain gloss on the Pataudi resignation stunt. The selection committee, says Bharatan, were due to discuss the manager's report before deciding the Captain for the Australia tour and Tiger wanted to pre-empt them. Bharatan writes:

> On the day he dropped that brick, Chandu Borde was in Bombay leading Maharashtra in the Ranji trophy. I rushed to his sea front hotel room at 7.00 in the morning to get his 'spot' reaction to the Pat bombshell. 'You look at last like getting the honour that was always rightfully yours', I said. 'Don't you believe it', said Borde, 'What's the bet he'll be back on the scene at the "psychological moment"? Don't get me wrong, this kind of thing's happened to me before. I was then promised everything and got nothing, I now just don't hope for anything. Don't believe all that you read. It's ultimately going to be Pat, and Pat alone, as Captain of India to Australia.'

Of course, in supposedly egalitarian, socialist India, Borde should have been the natural choice. He was one of ten children born into a family not very well off and a 'non-matriculate'. In the West the term may mean nothing, but in class and caste conscious India it immediately reveals a person's economic background. Matriculation is almost the minimum qualification most educated Indians aspire to and among middle Indians it is not uncommon to hear jokes that even their *peons* – office boys – are matriculate these days. Borde made it in cricket because of assistance from the Maharaja of Baroda, and later from the veteran Indian cricketer, Professor Deodhar. But in many ways, it was Borde's origins that told against him. A very popular story during Pataudi's reign was of the occasion when during a Test match, Chandu Borde decided to wear his Maharashtra cap and go out to field. Normally all Indian cricketers were required to wear their India cap during Tests. As Borde left the dressing room Pataudi told Borde that he was playing for India, not Maharashtra and should wear his India cap. Borde is supposed to have replied, 'But Tiger, you often wear your Sussex cap'. Tiger, looking down his long impressive nose, allegedly replied, 'Yes, Chandu, but Sussex is not Maharashtra.' There were different versions of this story with Tiger being credited with wearing the Winchester cap, or the Oxford cap, both of whom he captained. Again this may be an apocryphal tale, but one endlessly retold and with every retelling, Tiger acquired a new aura. The story, however unlikely, seems to combine all the Tiger qualities.

Tiger, himself, disarmingly acknowledges that he was made Captain because he was different. 'In fact I was selected because culturally and regionally I was from nowhere in particular. I was the simplest way out for our faction ridden Board. The Indian team is probably the hardest to captain anyway. First of all you are invariably the weakest side and then you could have the problem of dealing with twelve culturally, ethnically and linguistically different people.' Or to put it plainly, Tiger was India's 'great Captain' because he was a prince, a Nawab. We have discussed the role of princes in Indian cricket but Tiger was the last of the princely cricketers to play a part in Indian cricket. Some Indian sceptics would joke that Tiger was the 'Nawab of Kuch-be-Nahi', meaning the Nawab of nothing. This was a reference to the fact that Pataudi, which gave Tiger the title of Nawab, is a very small place just outside Delhi. As Indian princely stages go it is nothing more than a pimple. But that did not matter for what Tiger carried was the 'Nawabsahib'.

There are two words to denote princes in India. If the prince is a Hindu then he is generally called a Raja or a Maharaja, the second word meaning a greater Raja. If the prince is a Muslim then he is called a Nawab. In Tiger's case there was the aura of his father's Nawabsahib. The Nawab of Pataudi Senior had played for England, scoring a century in the 1932–3 Bodyline tour, and then captain-ing India on the 1946 tour of England. But even without such antecedents the very word Nawab would have created the right association for Tiger. We have spoken of the poor Muslims being the Indian 'niggers'. But however much the Hindus may resent, fear and mistrust the ghetto Muslims, they also carry with them the image of the other Muslims. The Muslims who ruled them and left behind the monuments of northern India, specially the Taj Mahal that is so eagerly exhibited to foreigners. Hindu historians may

138

endlessly debate the legacy of these Muslim rulers, but in the popular mind there is still respect and longing for the wonder of this Muslim rule.

This is the Nawabsahib. Nawabs were unpredictable but glorious, handsome but also cruel, capable of great generosity and of great wickedness. Their whimsy was part of their charm and everybody enquired what the Nawab's *mezaz* (mood) was like. The right mood could grant a thousand favours, the wrong could mean the end. The Nawab of Pataudi inherited much of this, other, Hindu feeling towards Muslims and very often when he took one of his more eccentric decisions it would be explained as 'Nawabsahib's mezaz'. This Indians, and Hindus in particular, knew from their own history was not something to be trifled with. In a sense by clinging to the concept of the Nawabsahib, alternatively capricious and glorious, Indians were trying to unite their very muddled history.

Apart from Pataudi no other Muslim cricketer has evoked this special feeling. This is hardly surprising since Pataudi and his father were the only two Muslim princes to play Test cricket for India, or for that matter Pakistan. Before Indian independence, and the partition which came in its wake, Muslims formed a sizeable proportion of the Indian Test team. Nearly all of them were from Punjab, a northern Indian state, and generally from the Indian middle classes. India's partition meant the division of Punjab, and the loss of a great many Muslim cricketers. Since then India has always had Muslim cricketers, and most Indian Test teams have fielded one, possibly two. But they have all come from the general Indian middle classes with the possible exception of the Indian wicket keeper Syed Kirmani, who describes his background as working class. In fact the only cricketer to remotely threaten Tiger as a romantic hero, a personage off as well as on the field, was another Muslim, Salim Durrani.

Here again there was something of the other Nawabi Muslim aura about Durrani. Salim is a magical name in India. It is the name that the Mughal Emperor Akbar gave to his son from his Hindu wife. Though Salim took the name Jehangir when he became Emperor, it was as Prince Salim that he created some of the most enduring Mughal legends. Legends strong enough to become translated into films like *Anarkali* and the epic *Mughal-E-Azam*. The name Salim evoked romance, valour and recklessness and Durrani's cricket symbolised all that. As N. S. Ramswami was to

139

write in an appreciation in *Indian Cricket*, Durrani broke hearts not records. Handsome enough to be lured by films, though not very successfully, there was always something very challenging about his cricket.

As an orthodox left-arm spinner he was not in the class of Bedi – more in the meaner tradition of Nadkarni but it was his approach to the game, particularly batting, that made Durrani special. 'We want six, we want six, Salim' the Indian crowd would shout and sure enough Salim Durrani, whatever the state of the game, would launch into one of his lovely, flowing drives and hoist the ball high over the bowler's head for a straight six. If India were struggling to save a Test, or win a tight game, commentators would often plead 'If only Salim gets his head down and plays responsibly, India could easily win this match'. Sometimes Salim did, many an occasion he did not. It all added to the great might-have-beens of Indian cricket. If only Salim would . . .

The Salim-Pataudi relationship was complex and interesting. Durrani was already established as a Test cricketer when Tiger made his debut. In the early years of Tiger's captaincy, Durrani's left-arm spin (Sobers found this particularly difficult) and middle order batting were quite crucial. By the mid-phases of Pataudi's captaincy it was clear that things were not working out well between them. I doubt if the fact that both of them were Muslims played any part in this. Tiger's hold on the Indian public was derived from the Nawabship, the ancestral royal blood that demanded loyalty from its subjects. Durrani's was the Bombay *filmi* charm: his slightly unkempt look – the long hair falling over the eyebrows and perpetually being brushed back – combined with his ability to convert lounging laziness into electric athleticism. I well remember the last occasion Salim Durrani played under Tiger's captaincy. It was the first Test of the 1966–7 series against the West Indies at Bombay. India, after a bad beginning, had struggled to make a decent score, with Durrani helping Borde in the rescue act. Durrani made a lovely fifty-five, including one huge straight six over Charlie Griffith's head into the CCI pavilion. If this was classic Salim, so was his dismissal, head in the air, bat askew and bowled by Sobers all over the shop. For much of the match he fielded at third man, just in front of the North Stand, and throughout the innings I seem to recall him combing his hair, wearing a rather detached, vacant look. Once or twice his preoccupation with his hair led him to misfield and one could almost feel the electricity passing between the Nawab of Pataudi and Salim Durrani.

India, through some bad catching and a dreadful batting collapse in the second innings, lost the Test. Durrani was one of the casualties. He was replaced by Bishan Singh Bedi. To most Indian cricket followers Bedi was unknown and to some his inclusion was seen as yet another example of the daftness of Indian cricket selection. Little did we know the magic in Bedi's left arm. But even after we appreciated it we continued to mourn Salim, though he did not make a comeback for almost five years. By then Pataudi had been replaced by Wadekar and nothing could comfort Indian cricket for the lost years of Salim Durrani.

There could be no such feeling about Abbas Ali Baig. In cricketing terms Baig came into prominence at about the same time as Pataudi and, in some ways, made even more of an impact. Baig played so well for Oxford in the 1959 season, that, when the main Indian batsman Vijay Manjrekar, had to withdraw because of a knee injury, the young Muslim cricketer was drafted in. He proved a splendid choice and was one of the few successes for the Indians on that dismal tour. Baig played in the fourth Test, after the Indians had lost the first three, and repeatedly hooked Trueman's bouncers. Though he was hit on the head by one bouncer, and had to retire hurt, he came back to complete a fighting century – joining a select band of Indians who had scored a century in their first Test.

Baig became an instant Indian hero. Here was a cricketer who could answer fire with fire, bouncers with hooks. His status as India's up-and-coming batsman was further reinforced the following winter when the Australians under Richie Benaud toured India. Though India lost the series, they won a Test match (their first victory against Australia) and Baig was a central figure in the Indian batting revival. In the third Test at Bombay, with India always struggling to stay in the match, Baig scored a fifty in each innings. Yet within a year Baig's cricketing world had been reduced to dust. After the 1959–60 Australian tour, he was to play just five more Tests for India in the next fifteen or so years. His nemesis came after his failure in the first three Tests of the 1960–1 series against Pakistan. His scores were: 1, 13, 19 and 1. Baig was dropped and did not play again for India until the 1966–7 tour of the West Indies when he played two Tests and was dropped.

Though he toured England with the 1971 team, he did not play another Test. Baig's low scores in 1960 and 1961 are difficult to explain, though not unusual. Other batsmen, even very great ones, have had seasons and series like that. What undid Baig was very simply that he was a Muslim playing for India against Pakistan.

The years 1960 and 1961 marked a watershed in India-Pakistan Test cricket. Test series between the two countries had started in the 1952–3 season, when India had won 2–1 at home. India had visited Pakistan in 1954–5 with all the matches ending in dreadfully dull, boring draws. The dull cricket did not make either country keen to have another visit and in any case after 1954 political relations between the two countries progressively deteriorated. Pakistan became more closely involved with American-sponsored alliances, while India became a champion of the non-aligned world.

Pakistan finally revisited India in the winter of 1960. The first Test was played in Bombay and was a sell-out long before it started. I persuaded my parents to let me visit the flat of one of their friends, which happened to overlook the Brabourne stadium. The route to the friend's flat passed Churchgate railway station and the entrance to the East Stand of the Brabourne stadium. On the first day of the Test I walked towards the flat and saw a whole crowd of very Muslim-looking people entering the stands. One passerby observed the rush of the Muslims and commented 'No wonder these *Meibhais* (as some Muslims are called) come crawling out now. It is their team that is playing. No prizes for guessing who they are supporting.'

This bitter remark reflected the feeling of many Hindu Indians during the series – that Muslims in India were all supporting Pakistan. It was this feeling that was to prove the undoing of Abbas Ali Baig. A failure in non-Pakistan series, or by a Hindu in that series, might have been overlooked. But against Pakistan the natural, albeit libellous conclusion was that Baig had sabotaged his own chances so that the good of Islam, in the form of the Pakistan cricket team, could triumph. Poor Baig heard so many whispers about his 'treacherous' behaviour and received so many poison pen letters that by the time he was bowled by Haseen for one in the second innings of the third Test in Calcutta, he was ready to throw in the towel. As *Current*, a review of India and Pakistan Test cricket between 1952 and 1984, puts it 'Confidence was further shaken by a torrent of poison pen letters, telephone

142

calls and telegrams. He opted out of the Indian team after the Calcutta Test.'

Baig never recovered from the libellous accusations made against him during that series. A one-down batsman who looked like becoming one of the Indian greats merely proved the Indian addage that batsmen who score a century in their first Test for India rarely score many more runs for India. It was a hoodoo that was to afflict Indian cricket until Viswanath broke the spell by scoring a century in his first Test and then going on to score a few thousand more runs.

As it was, the end of the 1960–1 Test series with Pakistan marked the beinning of an eighteen-year period when neither country played each other. Interestingly this was also the period when the two great Muslim cricketers that India has produced in the modern era, Pataudi and Durrani played for India. Neither Pataudi nor Durrani played for India against Pakistan. Had they done so we might have seen how their popularity and evident appeal would have stood the test of any possible failure. By the time India resumed cricket with Pakistan by touring the country in the winters of 1978–9, the only Muslim in the side was Syed Kirmani, and he was so established as a wicket keeper that few would dare to ascribe his failures to religious feelings. Even then, during the controversial Bombay Test of 1980–1, there were some mischievous whispers about Kirmani's loyalty. This, despite the fact that it was his stand of ninety-five for the seventh wicket with Kapil Dev, with Kirmani making a 'cheeky' forty-one, which helped India reach 334 in the first innings and played a crucial part in its victory.

But then it is hardly surprising. For Indian Muslims' relations with Pakistan complete the three-sided way in which Hindus view the Indian Muslim. There is the view of the katela, there is the Nawabsahib and then there is Pakistan. It is the interaction of the katela and the Nawabsahib with Pakistan that brings out all the old paranoia and distrust of Muslims. Physically India and Pakistan may be very close, but intellectually and emotionally, they are far apart.

In 1977 Pakistan had a traumatic election leading to the over-throw of Bhutto and the installation of General Zia al Haq. Yet the best reporting on Pakistan in the Indian papers was filed by Indian correspondents in London scavenging reports filed by British correspondents in Pakistan. News coming straight out of

Pakistan into India was almost invariably laconic agency dispatches that said very little. Nearly forty years after the sub-continent was split, Pakistan for most Indians is still not a living country. It is an ogre, a devil waiting to devour India, a fantastic mistake – but not a country of a hundred million human beings. I can remember very few articles which have talked of the people of Pakistan. Apart from the Indian news agencies there are hardly any Indian journalists based in Pakistan. Few visit the country. It is as if with the traumatic partition of the subcontinent something had snapped in the Indian mind. A limb of the body had been dismembered, it was said – and the body had forgotten that it had ever had this limb. Perhaps this was the only way in which the trauma of those days could be faced.

The long cricket break between India and Pakistan intensified this feeling. And though in recent years at least cricketing contacts have resumed, it is almost impossible to go from India to Pakistan. Those wishing to visit Pakistan invariably require a visa and the visas have to be issued in Delhi. In the early part of 1984 England visited Pakistan. I happened to be in India then and the Sports Editor of *The Sunday Times* thought it might be simpler for me to travel from Bombay to Karachi to cover the first Test. I soon realised the difficulties. I would have to go to Delhi to make a visa application, the Pakistani Embassy in Delhi would have to refer this to Islamabad and by the time the whole thing was settled, the first Test would be over. When I mentioned all this to my Sports Editor he was, understandably, bemused.

It was only when I began to live in England in the late 1960s that I overcame my ignorance and hostility towards Pakistan. This was largely through meeting Javed, who worked with me in a small, dingy, accountants' office just off Fleet Street, where we were both training to be chartered accountants. To Javed all Indians were Hindus and therefore despicable – which revolted my secular conscience about India being a nation for all religions. Javed would call me 'Indiana'. One of his minor hobbies was to pass himself off as a Mexican with his own version of an American accent. This mixture of Lahore English with a contrived New York accent produced some quite remarkable consequences.

When we first met we circled around one another warily, like two fighters in a ring waiting to land the first decisive punch. But all around us was this alien, white, English world – a world which could scarcely distinguish between Indian and West Indian, let

144

alone between Javed and me. Slowly we stopped circling and came to trust one another. Our friendship grew and seemed to be prospering when, suddenly, Pakistan unleashed its terrible repression of Bangladesh in the spring of 1971.

I was appalled to find Javed not only siding with Tikka and Yayaha Khans but despising the Bengalis in the sort of fascist rhetoric, which applied by a white to a black would have incurred all the wrath of the Race Relations Act. In my fading Bengali memory where ideas of a *sonar* (golden) Bengal still resonated, the Pakistani action was a heinous crime. The fragility of our friendship became even more evident as the repression continued through the summer of 1971. It was not helped by the fact that the Pakistani team just failed to beat England at cricket, while the Indians miraculously won a series against England for the first time in forty years. Javed felt that events were conspiring in my favour.

He was convinced of this when in December 1971 India and Pakistan went to war. While his Embassy told him, almost every day, how they had shot down hundreds of Indian planes with all Pakistani planes returning safely, British news media told a very different story. He was no longer the cool Mexican with his supposedly neat American accent. He began to look and sound a very angry Pakistani Peter Sellers. The Indians had cleverly allowed Western correspondents to report the war, and as their dispatches filled the media Javed, desperately needing to marry this with Pakistan's dispatches, began to believe in a great conspiracy embracing the BBC, all of Fleet Street and me. When the BBC showed the fall of the Bangladesh town of Jessore, he dismissed the pictures as belonging to a carefully camouflaged suburb of Calcutta. At the end of the war our relationship was in tatters.

It only recovered through the intervention of an external force; an Iranian who worked with us. He was junior to both Javed and me and would often try to butter up Javed by referring to him as 'my Muslim brother'. While the Bangladesh war raged Javed inclined to his Muslim brother. But after the war and the liberation of Bangladesh the Muslim angle began to wear thin.

The Iranian's English was rather poor and he often misunderstood things. He failed his very first accountancy exams because in the General Paper asked to write about the ways in which the English waterways system helped the transportation of goods, he had written about the Stock Exchange. It transpired that he had mugged up a certain number of questions and, not quite understanding what the word waterways meant, had taken it to refer to the Stock Exchange. Javed, on hearing his explanation, made malicious fun of his lack of English.

The breaking point came when one day Javed asked him to get the evening paper. Both Javed and I were very keen on cricket scores and in those days the *Standard* published a special late edition, available in Fleet Street some time after five, which contained the latest cricket scores. It had, I believe, the code number 7RR and Javed asked the Iranian to look for the number and make sure it had the latest cricket scores. But like the confusion between the English waterways and the Stock Exchange, this proved rather too much for him. He brought an edition which contained the lunchtime scores, which we already knew. Javed, furious, turned on him and said 'You are useless. You don't know the difference between the English waterways and the Stock Exchange or the difference between lunch and close-of-play scores.' The poor Iranian who knew nothing about cricket, did not know what to say and soon found that even liberal applications of 'my Muslim brother' did not mollify Javed. After that I was once again Indiana.

Perhaps this anecdote proves that cricket can override religious differences, bringing together people of very different backgrounds. Yet the history of India-Pakistan cricket, and the wider role of Indian Muslims in Indian cricket, suggests that even if it does, it does so in a somewhat unexpected way.

CHAPTER 8

Vegetarians, Fast Bowlers and Violence

If myth is the father of belief, then no belief is more mythical than the one about Indians being mild, meek and gentle. It is difficult to be precise as to when the West began to accept this myth but it probably dates from Victorian times, strengthened by the unique, non-violent approach used by Gandhi to fight the British. Indian conversations, discussions and even arguments have a certain elliptical, very decorous, manner. While Indians can be very inquisitive and very open about the most intimate matters, they often find it very difficult – or are reluctant – to say 'no' to situations which demand such an answer. They are more likely to say 'yes', or 'maybe' out of a quite unaccountable sense of inadequacy and, perhaps, in the hope that the problem will go away. This is allied to a severe dislike of what Victorians would have called 'robust language'.

In Great Britain, for instance, discussions or arguments be-tween friends – of a fairly standard nature – may feature phrases like 'What nonsense', or 'That's rubbish'. It does not mean the two friends are having a violent quarrel but merely a strong disagree-ment about certain things. But in India, even between intimate friends, the use of such language would very nearly threaten the friendship. I was reminded of this very sharply a couple of years ago when my nephew and niece, who live in India, visited me. During a discussion and disagreement, at one stage, irritated by what I thought was my niece's feeble arguments, I said 'Oh, what nonsense, come off it.' In a similar conversation with an English friend the remarks would have meant nothing. My niece was very upset and I had to spend much time and effort to mollify her and make her see that I did not mean it as a deep, wounding, personal insult.

It is this robust use of language by the West, particularly the English, that perhaps explains why in India the English have a reputation for being men, and women, of violent tempers. In

147

contrast, to the English, Indians seem meek and mild. However, the reality is very different. As Nirad Chaudhuri has explained in *The Continent of Circe* 'Few human communities have been more warlike and fond of bloodshed . . . Their political history is made up of blood-stained pages.' The Janus problem has arisen because of the oldest form of historical confusion: two disparate events have combined to produce a wholly misleading theory. The first, in the third century BC, concerned the conversion of a king. The second, in the twentieth century AD, concerned the politics of a Middle Temple lawyer. The King was Asoka, one of India's greatest kings and the shining jewel of the Maurya Empire of 300 BC. Asoka conquered a state called Kalinga in the course of which 50,000 people were deported, 100,000 killed and many times more died in other ways. It was as Nirad Chaudhuri says, an Assyrian method of warfare – total destruction. At the end of it, Asoka, seemingly overcome by remorse, proclaimed *ahimsa*, non-violence, as state policy. About twenty-five words, explaining the creed, were inscribed on massive iron pillars which were erected all over the country. Twenty-three centuries later the message re-emerged by means of a Middle Temple lawyer. Gandhi decided that *ahimsa* was the only way to fight the British. Asoka's declaration was good propaganda based on shrewd statecraft. He had conquered nearly all of India and there was no practical need for violence. Gandhi's decree was also good propaganda based on the shrewd realisation that an armed challenge to the British would be futile. But between these two events, as Chaudhuri says:

> There is not one word of non-violence in the theory and practice of state drafted by the Hindus. Read all the inscriptions, and you will find that when they are not bare records of gifts or genealogy, they are proclamations of the victories and the conquests of the kings concerned. The martial boasting is found not only among the Hindu Kings, but equally among the Buddhists . . . the whole of Sanskrit literature, from the epics down to the latest long poems, is full of accounts of battle and exultation of war and conquest. These were the business of Hindu Kings.

The Hindus developed the concept of the just war, *Dharma Yuddha.* The righteous war, and the events leading up to it, is the story of *Mahabharata,* which along with Ramayana, forms one of

148

the two great epics of Hinduism. The story of Mahabharata is a family row. The King dies, and the right of his sons to inherit his throne is challenged by his brother and his family. The brother's family, through evil means, occupies the throne and the rightful heirs seek justice. Finally, the two warring cousins meet in battle. But on the morning of the battle one of the dispossessed heirs expresses grave disquiet about the impending clash of arms. He cannot, he says, kill his own flesh and blood, the sons and nephews of his own uncle. But the God Krishna, charioteer to the reluctant warrior, launches into a unique exhortation to battle. The warrior is convinced and, eventually, after an epic struggle, righteousness prevails. Krishna's arguments constitute the *Bhagavat Gita*, Hinduism's holiest book. Unique, not only because of its philosophical arguments, but because it provides the only known case of war producing a religion's 'bible'.

The *Bhagavat Gita* has been interpreted as the great classic on the Hindu theory of acceptance and denial of free will. The violence that surrounded its birth provides the real clue as to how Indians see force, both in everyday life and on the cricket field. Ever since India made its entry on to the international cricket scene, it has been obsessed by the need for fast bowlers. Opponents repeatedly humbled India through pace particularly Hall, Gilchrist and Trueman. Every defeat increased the Indian obsession for an avenging fire. The great Hindu Goddess of strength is Kali and, for almost fifty years, Indians sought a Kali on the cricket field.

The post-1946 period has seen India produce some great spinners: Vinoo Mankad, Gulham Ahmad, Subhash Gupte, Bishen Bedi, Erapalli Prasanna, Venkatraghavan, Chandrasekhar. But though they are honoured and respected none of them evoked that special adulation that Kapil Dev conjured up. He personifies the long-cherished Indian dream of answering fire with fire, pace with pace, force with force. There is nothing meek or non-violent about him.

What aroused India was not only Kapil's good looks, or the sort of cavalier approach to batting that had been Salim Durrani's hallmark, but his bowling. For Indians it brings back hallowed memories of Nissar and Amar Singh, the two fast bowlers who opened India's attack in the country's first ever Test at Lord's in 1932. Though they opened the bowling in only six Tests, in Indian cricketing memory their names resonate in a manner similar to that of Hornby and Barlow in Lancashire, or Holmes and Sutcliffe in Yorkshire.

Both were very similar in looks – tall, strapping men, six feet two inches – though Mahomed Nissar was a Punjabi Muslim and Amar Singh was a Gujerati Hindu from Ranji's Nawanagar. Indeed, it was Ranji who spotted his potential rather early on. Kapil Dev is, probably, closer to Amar Singh in his cricketing outlook than Nissar. Amar Singh was not only a fine opening bowler, he was also a marvellous right-hand hitter whose clean stroke play could demoralise many an attack and quickly change the course of a match. Nissar and Amar Singh first came into prominence, or at least English notice, during India's inaugural Test at Lord's in 1932. England won the toss, Holmes and Sutcliffe who, a few days previously, had put on 555 runs for the first wicket, opened the batting. Within fifteen minutes of play both had fallen to Nissar and with Woolley run out, England were nineteen for three. Jardine had to play a major innings for England to reach 259, but Nissar ended the innings with 5 for 93. Amar Singh came into the picture in the second innings when his figures of two for eighty-four did not quite reveal the effect he had on the batsmen. While Nissar was a classical looking fast bowler both in action and style, he could swing the ball and break back viciously, Amar Singh, who had a rather shambolic run-up approach to the wicket, relied on swing and cut. In the heavier atmosphere of England it was his pace on the wicket which disconcerted batsmen and caused Wally Hammond to say that 'he came off the pitch like the crack of doom'.

According to one Indian cricket writer they 'formed one of the greatest double-edged opening attacks any country has turned on their opponents', ranking with such dread pairs of more modern cricket as Lindwall and Miller, Trueman and Statham, Hall and Griffith. The statistics hardly bear out such a contention. They did well enough in the thirteen Test innings in which they opened the bowling, all against England, taking fifty-three of the eighty-six wickets that fell. The Indians hyperbole reflects the despair and the near forty-year fast bowling famine that resulted after their departure. Both men were twenty-two when India made her Test debut at Lord's in 1932. They would have been in their prime at the time of the Indian tour of England in 1940. But that tour never took place and as Hitler's *Blitzkreig* laid waste to Europe, Amar Singh, suffering from an attack of pneumonia, died in Jamnagar. Though

Nissar lived on for another twenty-three years, India had lost its first, and only genuine, opening pair after a mere seven Tests.

The anguish, and hence the adulation for Nissar and Amar Singh, was all the greater because they had been preceded by other fast bowlers. According to one Indian writer 'it is a matter of eternal regret that India did not enter Test cricket in the early 1920s'. The regret may have come with hindsight but that era did seem to produce a great many fast bowlers. It is difficult to gauge their international position, but certainly the idea of club, college or national cricket teams, having opening bowlers with genuine pace was not quite so foreign to the contemporaries of Nissar and Amar Singh as they were to those of Mankard and Bedi in the 1950s and the 1960s.

This era marked the rise of the great Indian spinners and their prominence on the international stage. Inevitably in an attack dominated by spinners, to such an extent that even non-bowlers like Wadekar, Pataudi and Kunderan who was actually a wicket keeper opened the bowling, suggested certain arguable conclusions. India, so the belief went, was the land of spinners. The great Indian bowling gift was to produce small, gentle men who with guile, cunning and the intricacies of flight and spin deceived the batsmen. The hot climate, the slow pace of life, the contemplative nature of its people, all seemed to make this the land of mystery and spin a very natural one. Wickets were slow, the cricket was slow and in the boiling heat what could be more obvious than hour upon hour of spin patiently wearing down the batsmen.

That indeed was the picture in India through the 1950s, 1960s and for much of the 1970s. It is a picture that the Indians detested. Throughout this period the Indians mourned the loss of Nissar and Amar Singh and elusively searched for replacements. Indians hired overseas fast bowlers to try and unearth local talent. Alan Moss of Middlesex, Gilchrist, Stayers, King and Watson of the West Indies, all went out to India, all put young Indians through their paces, and all produced nothing.

As the years passed and the Indians were increasingly humiliated by pace – both at home and overseas – the memories of Nissar and Amar Singh glowed ever more brightly and the search for their replacement became ever more desperate. The Indian press regularly carried stories of 'lost' fast bowlers. Harrowing tales were told of how a promising fast bowler had been ruined by the misdeeds of the Indian Board. Even in the heyday of the great spinners the Indian Board was criticised for not including a token bowler who aspired to be quick. One critic wrote 'not even the encouragement of rubbing shoulders with the playing 11 at net practice on such occasions is available to youngsters aspiring to bowl fast'. Difficult though it was to see how a fast bowler could improve by rubbing shoulders with Bedi or Prasanna, the argument revealed the depth of feeling in Indian cricketing circles about the lack of fast bowling.

Such desperation could cloud the judgement even of sensible critics and make them doubt a spinner's worth even in the great victories against the West Indies and England in 1971. Perhaps this was because whilst India occasionally won through spin, it was pace, the pace of Trueman and Statham, of Lillee and Imran, of Hall and Gilchrist and almost any fast bowler that undid them. The images they had to live with was of their batsmen failing so dismally to cope with pace that their struggles became a joke. As for instance during the Trueman blitz of 1952 when an umpire is supposed to have said that what worried him during the series was not Trueman's bowling, but being trampled to death at square-leg by the retreating Indian batsmen. Sporting displays of fear are never pleasant and for Indians all the victories won by their spinners did not compensate for the terrible shame and humili-ation inflicted on their batsmen by opposing fast bowlers. Some of the critics pointed to India's slow pitches. But, neighbouring Pakistan, where the wickets were just as slow, if not slower, seemed to have an abundance of fast bowlers, or at least bowlers who could adequately open the innings. Some argued for a crash programme along military lines. The Indian military is held in high, if aloof, regard and there was at least one suggestion that Project Fast Bowler should be handed over to the army. As the most efficient thing in India, it would produce a workable solution. Others were more pessimistic and doubted whether it was in the Indian nature to produce fast bowlers. When one seemed to emerge Indian cricket writers went into raptures. The winter of 1967 saw one, Kulkarni, unexpectedly selected to tour Australia on the strength of one good spell of left-arm medium pace bowling on a sunny afternoon in Bombay. One cricket writer, overcome by this, immediately drew analogies between Kulkarni's selection and the West Indian selection of Ramadhin and Valen-tine for the 1950 tour of England. But while the West Indian hunch had proved marvellously right, Kulkarni, like so many other bowlers before him, proved a flop.

In the 1950s as the search for fast bowlers led to ever more bizarre ideas Vizzy suggested that the Punjab, where the men were supposed to be tall and brawny might be able to supply the goods. It was the granary of the country, it could become the workshop of the Indian fast bowlers. 'Give me ten Punjabis and I shall give you fast bowlers', Vizzy was supposed to have bragged.

The fact that Indians could readily believe that ten tall Punjabis could be taught to become fast bowlers, merely because they were tall, strapping lads, demonstrates the hunger of the cricketing public for a fast bowler. A desperation that made my school friends try and bowl like Lindwall and Bedser, and many Indians question the country's mental aptitude for cricket, and even the diet. Could a country that lived on rice and vegetables really produce fast bowlers to match those from countries that ate beef and pork? It was and is one of the most fascinating arguments in sports. Is vegetarianism an enemy of fast bowling? Fast bowlers need to be tall and strong, so ran the argument, then how could vegetarians with their supposedly puny bodies even match up to the demands of fast bowling?

Not all Indians are vegetarians. The Bengalis, living along the great rivers Ganges and Brahmaputra, and not far from the sea are voracious fish eaters. In fact the Bengalis differentiate between sweet-water, river fishes, which are a delicacy, and shun the salt-water sea fishes. Chicken and mutton are plentiful, even if mutton is somewhat misleading since what is consumed in India is goat meat, rather than lamb. But Hindus as a general rule do not eat pork and shun beef. The cow is worshipped as *Go-mata*, mother cow even if historians and philosophers debate whether this worship is actually part of Hindu religion or something that developed out of economic necessity. The view that beef-eaters are stronger than vegetarians is, I suspect, the legacy of Muslim and British rule. Beef, it began to be believed, gave them the strength to overawe and conquer the vegetarian Hindus.

I had illustration of this attitude a couple of years ago when I visited India with a friend Jim Pegg, Assistant Sports Editor of *The Sunday Times*. My father was already in poor health, unhappy with my decision to live away from home and discard the security and the riches of accountancy – for which I trained – for the risks of journalism. Always somewhat sickly he was now given to saying that he didn't have long to live and I should really give some thought to settling down – meaning marriage to a good Indian wife and life in a secure job in India. One day in order to reasure him I said, 'Baba I am sure you will live for a very long time. Look at Jim's mother. She is 93, twenty years older than you.' My father looked at me with a sadness that is still vivid in my memory and said, 'These people are different. They eat pork and beef. You cannot compare us Indians with them.'

It was an astonishing statement. A successful, well-travelled businessman his life had far from been a struggle and while he may not have eaten pork or beef his diet had hardly been wanting in any of the required vitamins. Yet even to him the mere tradition of eating pork or beef gave people strength and longevity. He looked so sad and forlorn that I did not have the courage to tell him that the latest medical research in the West showed that longevity was prolonged by avoiding red meat and eating fish – just the diet my father had followed all his life. A few months later when my father died, I recalled the conversation and realised the depths of his dejection.

Since then I have often heard such sentiments being expressed, if not in such extreme language but forcefully enough. And whenever the Indians suffer a trouncing at the hands of opposition pacemen the lament is heard that it is the lack of red meat in the diet that lets the Indians down.

Soon after the 1984 Olympics there was the all-too-familiar inquest about India's abject performance – a country of 800 million and not a medal to show for it. So great was the outcry against vegetarianism that the National Institute of Nutrition, Hydrebad, issued statistics to prove that Indian vegetarian food had just as much energy – if not more – compared to meats.

Lack of proper diet does explain the poor standard of the Indian physique. However, this is because for many Indians their diet is simply inadequate, not because they are vegetarians. Part of the Indian problem was that they ceased to believe that they could produce a fast bowler, capable of challenging the West. However Kapil Dev has proved, without doubt, that they can.

CHAPTER 9

Gods and Boys

'A boy', said Neville Cardus, 'looks upon his heroes at cricket with emotions terribly mixed. He believes they are gods, yet at the same time he has no real confidence in them. He thinks they are going to get out nearly every ball . . . Strangely indeed does a boy think that his favourite cricketers are the best in the world but still the most fallible and in need of his every devoted thought.'

Cardus was recalling his agonies as a child watching Lancashire. He loved Spooner so much he never dared to watch him make a stroke, 'I probably never saw him at the moment which he actually played a ball.'

Like Cardus I too have agonised about Indian cricket and can readily enter that special feeling, that mixture of joy and fear that is the foundation of sports enthusiasm. While age, maturity and experience do make one more cynical of joy and less frightened about fear it is part of sports watching, or at least partisan sports watching. Aside from Indian cricket my sporting loyalties are to Surrey and Tottenham Hotspur and come five o'clock on a winter Saturday evening a frisson of anticipation and fear passes through me as I await the result of Spurs. If it is right I am elated, if not depressed. As Colin Welland has said partisan sports watching is terrible; the price of the odd moments of bliss – and no bliss could be purer, as when Tottenham beat Liverpool at Anfield after seventy-two years – is years of frayed nerves and black moods.

This is not a particularly Indian thing. It is a universal phenomenon, which explains the emotions that sport can generate, also the almost mystical unity between sport and superstition. Don Revie always wore the same blue suit to football matches and I have sat for hours rooted to one uncomfortable spot in my living room, unable to move paralysed by fear that any change would mean the fall of an Indian wicket, or a goal against Tottenham. When on that magical day at the Oval in August 1971, Chandrashekar ran through England I stood rooted at one spot, not daring to move even for a pee, till the deed was done. It made me feel I played some part in it, though no doubt millions of Indians felt the same way. It is like being part of a magic spell, recreating a mythical time that has elapsed and will never return. Human history is rooted in myth and magic and sport is the twentieth-century way of recreating something that was part of our ancestors' lives.

Myth and magic are still central to Indian life, in a way that would appear exotic in the West. Serious newspapers can review alleged books of history that seek to prove that in prehistory Indians had an empire that included Britain. I once met the author of one of these history books and was told entertaining 'evidence' in support of such a theory. Asked why nobody else seemed to acknowledge or even mention it, he said, 'those pages of history have been forgotten'.

According to Dr Sudhir Kakar, a psychotherapist in New Delhi 'the world of magic and animistic ways of thinking lie close to the surface' in India. 'There seems', he says, 'to be a different relationship to outside reality, compared to one met with in the West. In India it is closer to a certain stage in childhood when our outer objects did not have a separate, independent existence but were intimately related to the self and its affective states. They were not something in their own right but were good or bad, threatening or rewarding, helpful or cruel, all depending on the person's feelings of the moment.'

V. S. Naipaul has borrowed this to argue that Indians have a childlike perception of reality and, unlike the West, cannot describe the sex act. To them 'it happened'. Naipaul using Kakar makes such of the fact that in his autobiography Gandhi never refers to landscape despite his travels to England, South Africa and in India. He was too busy coping with his own turmoil produced by these travels to be able to actually describe them.

The Naipaulian point is part of a wider thesis, what may be called the Naipauls' (both V. S. and his brother Shiva) view of India. That it is a wounded civilisation, whose intellectual ability is second rate and which has nothing to offer the world except its Gandhian concepts of holy poverty and its recurring crooked comedy of holy men and, while asserting its own antiquity, needs the West for every practical assistance.

This is perhaps a more brutal, less charmingly expressed version of a theory put forward by Nirad Chaudhuri that Indians are really Europeans, in thrall to the goddess Circe. The goddess with the flowing tresses, sweetly singing before her loom has drugged Indians into forgetting their European heritage.

Chaudhuri, in the tradition of great eccentrics, suggests that if only Indians rediscovered 'our original European spirit and character' and conquered the Indian environment all would be well.

Perhaps so. I cannot accept that the Indian intellect is second rate, or that Indians need to be Europeans – in any case the type of Europeans Chaudhuri has in mind are so idealised that they are rarely found outside books. What is necessary is a greater perception of reality. But that, at least in the sporting sense, is not merely an Indian failing. In fact it is most evident in this country during the Wimbledon fortnight. Britain puts on the greatest tennis show on earth but British players fail dismally to make much of a show themselves. Yet every Wimbledon involves the same ritual anticipation and hope in the media about the British hopefuls followed by anxious, almost tearful reporting of their defeats; as one commentator said we seem to watch an endless succession of Annabels being beaten by foreigners to be succeeded by much hand-wringing and despair about Britain's failure to produce players whose tennis ability matches the organisational ability of Wimbledon.

Something similar happens in Indian sports. Like the British tennis aficianado Indians collect the little nuggets of success, treasure them and return to them again and again puzzled and worried as to why they have not led to the sporting pot of gold that has been promised. Listen to this interview with Vijay Amritraj, published just before the 1985 Wimbledon. When Amritraj first emerged on the scene he was linked with Borg and Connors as the ABC of tennis. 'We find that B and C have done quite well,' asked the interviewer. 'What about you?' Amritraj frankly confesses that he was never in the same class and that 'it is not always that if you have three children they would perform equally well given the same opportunity'.

Yet the question betrays both the hope and despair of the Indian sports follower. A promising player emerges, the world press writes some favourable words about him, Indians immediately treasure this as an omen for the future and, when it does not materialise, bemoan their fate, the champion who has failed and the world in general. When Ramanathan Krishnan, the greatest tennis player India has produced was at his prime, pre-Wimbledon articles in the Indian press invariably asked, 'Can Krishnan win Wimbledon?' He never did, though he was in two semi-finals and Indians took what solace they could from lyrical articles, by Geoffrey Green and others, rhapsodising about the Indian's artistic touch-play. It was almost a touchstone of reassurance, something to cling to. It was much later when I read Geoffrey Green's autobiography that I realised how much of a spell India, itself, had cast on certain writers.

All this has made the Indian sports enthusiast at once a hunter of nuggets about India's sporting achievements, and quite the most wide-eyed observer of the international sporting scene. Partly because of the corrosive colonial influence, partly because Indian sports journalism lacks confidence and very often substitutes coverage of home sports with reprints of articles from the English press, the Indian sports enthusiast, compared to an English one, is astonishingly well-informed about the major English and international sports. He can comment intimately in a manner that would quite baffle most Englishmen.

Here is Akhilesh Krishnan, from Madras, in a letter to *Sportsweek*, about Martin Crowe playing for Somerset (15 February 1984):

> It is a real bonus for Somerset to sign the gifted New Zealand batsman Martin Crowe for this year's English County Championship matches. Crowe celebrated his selection with a timely 100 in the first Test at Basin River (sic), Wellington. Crowe came in place of West Indian Vivian Richards and hoped to do well as an all-rounder. During New Zealand's England tour last year Crowe registered an average of over 50 in county matches and claimed useful wickets as a medium-pace bowler. Incidentally in the first Test against England at Wellington, Crowe's elder brother and Auckland captain Jeff Crowe top scored in the first innings and his younger brother followed it up with a defiant century. Thus, the brothers played a stellar role in salvaging the reputation of the Kiwi team. Only the Chappell brothers have done better than the Crowe brothers in Test cricket. It is a real boon for New Zealand cricket and Somerset to have such a fine utility player.

All countries develop their eccentrics who know a great deal about one particular foreign country. But in India such eccentrics are the norm, and during the summer of 1984 as Gower and England lurched from defeat to defeat against Clive Lloyd's West Indians, the Indian sporting press was full of articles from sports reporters confidently opinionating about events of which they had little direct knowledge.

One can see the colonial hangover, though I have seen Indians express similar opinions about events in Russia or even America – and not merely in sport. It is part of the tremendous Indian facility – something they share with Latins – of developing a quick and easy intimacy with places and people that may appear intrusive, or even rude to the Anglo-Saxon but seems most natural to the Indian. The obverse of this is that Indians themselves are tremendously susceptible to flattery, particularly if the flatterer happens to be a foreigner, and a white one, at that.

It was something well appreciated by Tony Greig during the 1976–7 England tour of India, so well indeed that he used the Indian crowds to help him inflict a crushing defeat on the Indian team, and in Robin Marler's memorable phrase became the Clive of cricket. Greig's achievements on that tour were indeed something out of fiction, transforming his team which, on paper was weaker than the Indians, into world-beaters by using what should have been the opponents' best weapon: support from the home crowd. Before the tour few could have imagined it.

A South African-born Englishman, the very epitome of the blond Anglo-Saxon, going to a coloured country and proving such a great hero that, even as he inflicted a crushing defeat on its national cricket team, he was idolised by millions of natives. Yet Tony Greig did just that in India during that winter Test series.

On the field, he inflicted one of the worst defeats ever sustained by India at home; off the field he advertised towels, creams for chapped skins, ointments for bruised ankles and even the awful Indian blades, proving that sexual appeal is not dimmed by a change of climatic zones. Calcutta's Grand Hotel where the MCC stayed, was virtually immobilised by hundreds of Bengalis screaming to get a glimpse of 'Taani', while even as India won a solitary Test at Bangalore, women of this supposedly arch-conservative southern city flashed their considerable bell-bottomed trousered legs at Greig. As one Indian journalist put it, 'He beat our men, took our money and screwed our women', and that from a modern cricketer is something.

Much of what he did would have been banal in England, dismissed in that classic Brian Johnston phrase, 'Greig is doing his nut.' If he beat a batsman he would raise his arms and keep

159

them raised for a minute; if he stopped a ball he would go down on his hands and knees and pause. Once he cover-drove Bedi, going down on his left knee, and remained frozen for almost a minute, much to Bedi's annoyance. Standing at silly point, he would flex his muscles and bring a roar from the crowd, or he would turn to them and pointing at the batsman shake his knees, capturing the batsman's uncertainty.

But his gestures were discriminating, distinguishing between populist expectations and élitist tastes. In India the cheaper stands are all to one side of the ground, generally known as the East Stand. Here great masses of people are herded in like cattle – and a single movement can cause whole ranks to sway. For hours they stay rooted to one spot, ready with tiffin carriers and makeshift potties (generally empty coconuts).

When the cricket becomes boring, incidents are generated; and often during the course of a day's play there are huge roars to relieve boredom, and totally unrelated to the game. In front of the simple medieval crowd Greig performed antics which one English journalist, apologising for his fuddy-duddy image, opined no English Captain should indulge in. His favourite one was to indicate a shapely woman by rubbing the ball on his breast in a manner that was unmistakable.

For the affluent sections, which invariably included the press and players' enclosures, Greig would doff his cap or wave and smile – gentle, appropriate gestures, to a crowd aware of its own status as the leaders of modern thrusting India.

Greig's task was made easier by the fact that Bedi, the Indian Captain was a Sikh, and subject to Irish-style comic jokes, the 'Sikh twelve o'clock'. Once a promising Sikh cricketer dropped a sitter at precisely twelve o'clock and was so devastated by the subsequent sarcastic attacks that ultimately he retired from the Test scene.

Then in the wake of the Sanjay Gandhi-led family planning programme, a popular joke had been going the rounds. One day a very worried Sikh returns home and tells his wife, 'You know, our son is doing very badly at school. Four years ago he was in the seventh standard (roughly equivalent to the first form). Then the teacher said that he was not up to it and he was demoted to the fifth standard. Last year to the fourth standard and this year to the third standard. If this goes on it is going to become dreadful and you'd better watch out. Tie your clothes very tightly round yourself because otherwise, who knows, he may one day suddenly re-enter your womb.'

Bedi, with his idiosyncracies, accentuated this. He always emerged ten or fifteen minutes after the lunch and tea sessions of play had commenced (the joke ran: he was still in the loo) and all this emphasised Greig's stature.

So while Bedi was often the butt of jokes, Greig was the subject of poetry, much of it terrible. In Calcutta's popular stands he was called Greigda – a Bengali term of respect used for the older brother – which was itself some measure of the growing self-confidence of the Indian crowds. Not so long ago he would have been called Greig sahib, which is the proper term of respect for a white man, or any distinguished man in these parts.

Watching Greig on the field one began to believe in superman. From the moment he led his team on and made them bow to the crowd in the manner of a football side, you felt you were in the presence of a conjurer, his magic made possible by the receptiveness of the Indian crowds.

But though Greig's visit was deeply humiliating – and as an Indian reporting for the English media I experienced at first hand the cruel spell the white man can still cast over my fellow Indians, often at my own expense – it also marked a development in Indian crowds. *Greigda* was the cry of a Calcutta crowd that was no longer happy with the dreary draws of the 1940s and 1950s. Indian cricket, or at least its supporters, had moved into the second, more demanding phase of the game.

Dr Richard Cashman has identified four phases of Indian cricket: 1932–6 when India played seven Tests, lost five, used twenty-six players: 1946–59 when India won her first ever Test: 1959–69, when Ramchard, Contractor and mostly Pataudi rebuilt Indian cricket and introduced a positive outlook and 1971–9 (his book was published in 1980) when India won Test series in England and the West Indies for the first time and the spin quartet of Bedi, Chandrashekar, Prasanna and Venkat came to the fore.

The classifications make some sense but I would personally define three phases of Indian cricket.

The first, the colonial phase lasted from 1932–71 when, despite some victories and a sea-change in attitudes brought about by Pataudi, Indian crowds did not expect to win. They were happy enough with performances which stretched opponents, and brought the team good notices even if they ended in failure. But all that changed in 1971.

The transformation was all the sweeter because it was so sudden and unexpected. Before the Indians went on that West Indian tour in the winter of 1971 Pataudi was deposed as Captain – a fact that hardly encouraged the Indians to think they could take on the mighty West Indians. Certainly not the new captain Ajit Wadekar who, before the crucial selection committee meeting, was not even sure he would be selected to tour. In fact Wadekar told Pataudi that he hoped Pataudi would use his influence to see that he made the tour. Pataudi who probably sensed what was coming replied, that it was more likely that he, Pataudi would require Wadekar's help to get selected when Wadekar became Captain.

So the Indians left Bombay, in John Woodcock's memorable phrase, with a couple of useful spinners, not including Chandra-shekar – he joined later for the England tour – and in six months were being talked about as world champions. This was probably not as outlandish a claim as some English critics seemed to think. India beat the West Indies in the West Indies – albeit a weak West Indian side – and then England in England, an England that under Illingworth had looked invincible and had just won back the Ashes in Australia.

Yet even at the beginning of the English tour Indians had to pinch themselves to believe that here at least was a team that could fulfil their fantasies. From the first day of the Lord's test it was clear that the Indian spinners would trouble England. When India took the first innings lead in the Test it was the first time in forty years of Test cricket in this country and the euphoria was understandable.

It was also tinged with a feeling that it was just too good to last and I well remember the reactions of the Indian supporters on the last day of the Lord's Test. India having bowled out England were left 183 to win their first ever Test in this country in four hours and twenty minutes. A chase particularly against the weather, but attainable and after losing two quick wickets Engineer and Gavaskar, in their very different ways, set about getting it.

I sat next to a West Indian whose drinking matched his exuberance. 'Man, you are going to win. Man you are whipping England.' I was not so sure and the Indians around me were even more uncertain. Every time Engineer dashed down the wicket to Gifford the Indians held their breath – they knew their Faroukh, they knew how fickle their cricket gods could be. By the time rain set in at tea, India required thirty-eight to win with two wickets left. My West Indian friend had long since vanished and the caution of the Indian supporters was justified. Certainly the Indians overdid the world champions hype after the Oval victory but when you have waited quite as long as that to savour success you are entitled to some over-reaction.

The more significant effect was that after these victories Indians began to get a taste for them, the generation fed on draws at home and defeats abroad was a philosophical one – they didn't expect much and were thankful for what they received. But after 1971 the supporters' expectations changed; they greeted victories with theatrical euphoria and defeats with depressing fury. Thus when the Indians lost all three Tests in England in 1974, being bowled out for forty-two at Lord's, there was such fury against the Captain Ajit Wadekar and the manager Hemu Adhukari that they chose to return to the country quietly – long after the team had gone. Even before they left England for home the team had discovered how fickle supporters can be. On the golden 1971 visit nearly all the Indians in England seemed to want to socialise with them. In 1974 after the forty-two all out at Lord's the invitations dried up so quickly that the bereft players began courting the despised journalists – more so after they were snubbed by the High Commissioner which provoked a tremendous backlash against the cricketers in India.

Indians, perhaps, more than most people can veer from one extreme to another and this phase certainly saw the development of some unpleasant ruthless behaviour such as in the sacking of Wadekar whose record as India's Captain though brief – only three Test series – is quite the best. The Indians had discovered that their newly-created gods had clay feet.

In 1983 the Indians won the World cup which marks the start of the third phase of Indian cricket. Between 1932–71 Indians regarded a draw as a victory, 1971–83 introduced them to the heady delights of victory and made defeat that much more difficult to accept. The World cup triumph of 1983 delightful as it was, was also something of a trap. It made Indians think that they ought to win every match, and they began to believe their own propaganda of being world champions of one-day cricket. While there is some substance in this, in that since the World cup, India has won limited overs tournaments in Sharjah and Australia, it is significant that these triumphs have all come away from home.

At home the Indian record is more patchy and some of the blame for this must fall on the Indian crowds. As Sunil Gavaskar said after the Indians' triumph in Australia in the winter of 1984-5, at home the crowds create such pressure with their relentless expectations that they unsettle the players and force them to play in a virtual pressure cooker with inevitable loss of form and motivation. Crowds that once applauded draws, now find even the hint of defeat difficult to stomach.

This has been accentuated by the fact that the World cup triumphs came in one-day matches where there are no draws. It has made one-day matches all the rage and so depressed the worth of Test matches that, apart from Calcutta, none of the Tests on England's last tour generated much interest.

The explanation for this is perhaps that what had been taken as genuine enthusiasm for cricket was instead *tamasha* – a wave of emotion and feeling. Indian political analysts often describe elections in terms of waves, the 'Indira wave' for the 1971 elections, the 'anti-emergency wave' for the 1977 elections, the 'sympathy wave' for the 1984 post-Indira Gandhi elections. Cricket enthusiasm too can be described in terms of waves. It developed in the mid-1960s and grew on the back of the 1971 victories and the spread of radio and television coverage. The World cup victory shattered the Test wave and replaced it with a frenzy for the new one-day stuff which seemed to better suit both pockets and social tastes.

In his autobiography, *Tiger's Tale* Pataudi still seeing India with the sense of wonder that Winchester and Oxford had instilled in him, wrote, about Indian cricket crowds of the 1950s and 1960s thus: 'Cricket in India today is non-spectacular low-key stuff played on shirt front sunbaked wickets. The crowds do not seem to mind at all. They lap it up. It may be another fifteen years before they become sophisticated and outspoken in their demands for more action and better results but it will happen.'

Tiger's prediction has come true, though perhaps not quite in the way he imagined. India has a wonderful facility of making fools of futurologists – it is a Western game that sits uneasily in India. It is easy both for Indians and Westerners to be swept up by Indian enthusiasms and come to extravagant conclusions. Despite the undoubted progress that the country has made, Indians show no sense of history or analysis. As technology improves, as middle India became stronger, even attempts at elementary analysis recede, confusing both Indians and foreigners. I can easily see why Scyld Berry should have made his confident prediction that India was destined to become the international cricket capital in 1982 but now sounds much more chastened after the somewhat different experiences of 1985.

I recall talking to Raj Singh, manager of the Indian team to England in 1982 and a shrewd observer of the game. The Indian tour began disastrously, India losing the one-day matches against England but Raj Singh was philosophical. The one-day game was foreign to India. Let England play this rubbish. We Indians, he said, would stick to the real thing – the Tests. Yet even as he spoke India was entering its most barren Test period – thirty-one Tests without a win before India beat England at Bombay in the winter of 1984 and its greatest, most glorious moment in international cricket was just a year away in the World cup.

Raj Singh, like Scyld Berry, was basing himself on what seemed to be unmistakable pointers. A large and growing urban population extremely fond of the game, vast facilities including stadia that dwarf most in England and the spread of radio and television, particularly ball-by-ball commentaries on radio in Indian languages that, Raj Singh, felt, had made the game Indian. The commentaries are awful, the commentators very often selected by the Minister of Information on a jobs for the boys basis but Raj Singh's point has validity. Above all there is the climate which for most of the year is rainfree. All signs that seemed to bear out Scyld Berry's assertion in *Cricket Wallah* in 1982 that Indian batting would always remain orthodox 'because the one-day game, which grows fast in other Test countries, holds no great attraction'. The winter of 1981–2, in fact saw India play their first one-day international at home.

The World cup transformation came about because of the deeds of a group of highly motivated north Indians led by Kapil Dev. But it was a transformation wrought by individuals – as had always been the case in India – and it is this that makes any prediction about Indian cricket hazardous.

Cricket owes its growth in India to certain individuals – Parsees, keen to become British, the princes keen to preserve their archaic rule nourishing it as a way to curry favour with the British, and now the businessmen and industrialists of middle India who see in it vast opportunities for commercial profit. For two decades the profit potential lay in Test matches but now that the focus has shifted to one-day matches one can see that the old theory of India being the last bastion of Test cricket has little to support it.

Unlike England, Indian cricket has not developed the roots through village and club cricket that sustain the English game whatever the merits of the national team. Unlike the West Indies it is not a nationalist factor that brings together the disparate islands. Indians do not play cricket to further their national sense of identity – they suffer from a surfeit of such symbols.

Indians themselves recognise that they have failed to develop some of the attributes that form a cricketing or sporting culture. Indian defeat led to inquests about cricketers' lack of the 'killer instinct'. Almost believing their own propaganda that Indians are artistic touch-players who are a bit too gentlemanly for their opponents, Indians endlessly debate about how they might acquire the ruthlessness that marks out a Connors or McEnroe. The foreigners' rhapsody about Indian gentleness is used as a stick to beat the failed cricketers.

Perhaps the problem is that Indians expect too much from their cricketers – expectations aroused by the generally low standards of reporting and analysis of the game in the country. Despite the growth and development of the game, India has yet to develop the sort of cricket journalism common say, in England or Australia. It is very common for a series of Test matches in the same newspaper to be reported by different journalists reflecting the different regions of the country.

Of course development of proper cricket journalism has hardly bothered the West Indies but India, where the game is constantly compared to England or Australia, reinforces cricket tamasha-fiesta. A fiesta can take many forms, it can fluctuate from day to day, even from event to event and there are signs that this is just what Indian cricket is doing.

This would suggest that the Indian temperament is more suited to football which even as played in the West is more of a fiesta, less analytical and formal than cricket. Football, as we have seen, remains the most popular sport in India. England's cricketers witnessing the decline of spectator interest in Tests during the last tour were surprised to find the enthusiasm for football – a game they thought was foreign in India. What it has lacked, outside pockets such as Bengal, is social acceptance and the political patronage given to cricket. But if interest in Test cricket slides, and one-day cricket does not quite fill the vacuum, then one can see football reclaiming the role that Vivekananda proclaimed for it all those years ago. Football has many hurdles to overcome, not least the tremendous Indian ability to introduce politics into everything, but if it can it may be just possible to see India become the football capital of the twenty-first century.

India, said R. K. Narayan, will always go on. Indian cricket too will survive but the form it will take may surprise many. Enthusiasms wax and wane in India perhaps more so than in other countries and there are definite signs that the enthusiasm for Test cricket so strong in the 1960s and 1970s has now begun to wane. One-day cricket has replaced it but fortune is fickle and Indians could soon discover another tamasha to amuse and titillate them. I hope it does not happen, but I fear it might.

CHAPTER 10

My India, My England

This book began with a question, India, whose India? It is not entirely for the sake of symmetry that I seek to conclude with a personal perspective on both India and cricket. 'There was a time', wrote V. S. Naipaul in *India – A Wounded Civilisation,* 'when Indians who had been abroad and picked up some simple degree of skill said that they had been displaced and were neither of the East nor the West. In this they were absurd and self-dramatizing: they carried India with them, Indian ways of perceiving. Now, with the great migrant rush, little is heard of that displacement. Instead Indians say that they have become too educated for India. The opposite is equally true: they are not educated enough; they only want to repeat their lessons. The imported skills are rooted in nothing; they are skills separate from principles.'

Of course it is always easy to criticise but Naipaul has a point. Who speaks for India? Can I, who have lived much of the last seventeen years in England – having left India when I was 21 – really write about India, her society or even her cricket? In India I am alternatively seen as a well-off Indian who can be sponged on during a visit to London, or a traitor who has abandoned the sweet poverty of India for the riches of the West. Like Anthony de Mello's implied criticism of Ranji some of my Indian friends think that the reason for my self-chosen exile is a romantic involvement. In fact I would probably have a better life-style in India, I could certainly afford servants which I cannot in North London. Indians, particularly rich Indians, exalt poverty – not their own but the concept of poverty and want to believe that anyone choosing the West in preference to India must have been seduced by its material comforts. In my case the reverse is true since, as I explained, middle India, to which I belonged is about the most material place on earth.

I was forcefully made aware of the mixture of scorn and lust that Indians have for *pardesis* – Indians living abroad – during my coverage of the Rajendra Sethia story, the Indian-born British businessman who eventually became the world's biggest bankrupt and is currently in jail in India awaiting extradition to this country.

168

At the height of the story I was visited in my London offices by an Indian doctor practising in Harley Street, who claimed to be a friend of Rajendra Sethia and who told me that as an Indian, and a fellow Bengali, I should stop writing about Sethia's business exploits. I was harming the Indian business community in London and did I really want to help the white men finish off this outstanding Indian businessman.

In England I have become in the words of a friend of mine the second best Indian professional – Salman Rushdie being the first. As interest in India has revived and Raj nostalgia seems to be the vogue, I find myself asked to become the expert on almost everything Indian from books, to fashion, festivals, cinema, food and, of course, cricket. Within minutes of Mrs Gandhi being shot, I was on the air explaining what it meant and how things might develop. Occasionally it can be tiring. It is one thing earning money pretending to be an expert in all things Indian – it is another constantly advising friends and acquaintances which Indian take-away they should frequent but the pleasures outweigh the problems. It is certainly better than being asked by Indian newspapers to write for next to nothing – merely for the love of India.

I sometimes even become enough of a professional Indian to find myself aroused by some slight to India or Indians. When I first arrived in this country my Indian nationalism was pristine. Though born eight months before the British left India and brought up in a mixture of cultural traditions – large doses of P. G. Wodehouse and William Brown, queueing up to see the Queen, yet hailing Mahatma Gandhi as the father of the Indian nation – I, like most of my contemporaries, held the British responsible for India's problems. My contemporaries who have remained behind in India have grown ever more nationalist and bitterly anti-British, fed on a constant stream of stories of the behaviour of immigration officers. I find that apart from my loyalty to the Indian cricket team, and some personal ties, my links are less secure. I still retain my Indian passport – India does not allow for dual nationality – and though I am a resident in this country it causes the odd niggle every time I enter and leave. I could take a day trip to France – for which I require a visa – and still be asked by the immigration officer, 'Are you still resident here?' I can think of a million answers but I merely say, 'Yes.'

When I came to England I had hoped to lose myself in the

cosmopolitan world of London, but I find that I cannot. Perhaps as Naipaul says Indians do not understand the word cosmopolitan – it was a word much used in my childhood to describe Bombay. We meant Bombay was cosmopolitan in that it contained the different Indian communities which perhaps betrayed how we saw the Indian nation. London is indeed cosmopolitan but it is also English and I occasionally tire of those well-meaning English acquaintances who, trying to make me feel at 'home', enquire whether I 'eat everything' and solicitously ask my opinion about the latest Indian fad. That blonde who wants to see *Passage to India* with me – is she interested in me or in keeping up with Raj nostalgia; that editor who says we must talk about the Raj revival, is he offering me work or just keeping himself informed about different views?

But all exiles must feel that, except perhaps English exiles who seem to have a remarkable ability not only to carry their England intact with them, but impose it on others. My India crumbles every time I visit India, and I am very like an Israeli friend of mine who has similar feelings about his country – I look forward to going 'home', but often hate it while I am there. I resent Indians trying to label me as pro-Indian or anti-Indian like children playing with the toy of nationalism and I am often confused by my own reactions to my own country. This was vividly brought home to me some years ago.

Some time before I left England I, along with a group of theatrical friends, had put on a show called 'The Black Man's Burden', or, to give its more graphic subtitle, 'It Gets Dark Earlier Since They Came'. After the first night the thing was thrown open for discussion. Somebody opinioned that the British reaction to India was the result of the brutalisation they had gone through as a result of climate, behaviour of natives and many other factors. I believe the man was Indian, though he had a rather English-looking wife who seemed embarrassed by his question. Nettled, I reacted angrily and played the part of the aggrieved Indian nationalist with some effect. Three months later I was in Calcutta's main street – Chowringhee.

My watch strap had broken and I had it repaired from a fairly established place. The service was courteous, I was given a bill (which has to be asked for in India) and I was reassured about the guarantee. A few days later the strap broke in very peculiar circumstances – it fell into the loo. The watch was damaged and I decided to go back to the shop. Three months had taught me a lot and I quickly worked out my strategy. The moment I entered the shop my voice was well above reasonable complaining terms and without any preliminaries I demanded to know the name of the shopkeeper's solicitor. The man, obviously puzzled and dreadfully worried, tried to mollify me: he smiled, he shook his head, he walked up and down behind his counter; with folded hands and head bowed he walked all round me; he offered me a chair. I refused to budge from the straight and narrow legal path. 'I want to know the name of your solicitor.' Even as he replaced the strap, repaired and serviced the watch and even the glass case – all at no expense – I stood fuming. As I left the shop, he smiled and bowed and I was convinced of the virtue of behaving occasionally like a colonial satrap. Later, when I wrote about it to a friend I made the point that had so nettled me in London: this is the inevitable result of living among an élite that has adopted and preserved the worst instincts of its colonial masters. The cycle was complete. Philosophically unreconciled to India, physically part of it.

Every Indian, says Naipaul, sees himself as unique, to be the only one of his sort to be recognised abroad. Nehru was often described – and liked being described as the lonely aristocrat. Aristocracy is easy in India as the English cricketers have often discovered and Tony Lewis realises every time he visits the country, instantly surrounded by Indians who still recall his captaincy of the England tour of 1972–3. I have no illusions about my uniqueness or of being an aristocrat. English friends of mine have suggested I straddle two cultures. I doubt that – I merely exist in the slipstream of both, one ruled by caste and money and the other by class and accent.

Caste and money are the great arbiters of Indian society just as class and accent divide the English. Caste is a more invisible barrier in India than people in the West think. You cannot tell Indians' caste by their looks and in modern, middle India, people of different castes live side by side, eat together, club together, play sport together and often do business together. Where they draw the line is marriage – then the many myriad caste and sub-caste distinctions surface to preserve the ancestral barriers. Unlike the West integration in India stops on the threshold of the bedroom.

Outwardly class is more manifest in England and signified, very often, by accent. I did not realise the variety and importance of accent in England until I arrived in this country. Brought up on the 'export only' version of English, I thought everybody spoke like Brian Johnston or Alvar Liddell. John Arlott didn't, but then he was the equivalent of God giving ball by ball commentary, and I can still recall the chill in my spine as that unique voice conveyed the fear of Indian batsmen facing up to the menace of Trueman. I could almost imagine them getting out before Trueman had approached the crease. To me, as to most Indians, the Scots, the Irish and the Welsh existed in the jokes told by the English but they were not separate entities.

This idea of an English stereotype who always wore a three-piece suit whatever the weather, and read *The Times,* is even now prevalent in India and one reason why Don Mosey, the BBC's cricket commentator, found life a shade difficult in India during the 1981–2 tour of the country. The Indians were just not used to BBC correspondents who did their commentaries dressed in beach shorts and spoke in a Yorkshire accent. I can well recall the conversation of a group of Indians who encountered an English-man visiting India during the India versus England series and could not understand why he was not interested in the score or English cricket fortunes. 'But isn't he worried about how his country is doing?' asked the puzzled Indians.

The English do have great pride in their country – as they have every reason to – despite the self-deprecatory air they normally adopt. But this pride surfaces as patriotic fervour only when England play Australia at cricket, Scotland at football or the Welsh at rugby. Then my English friends seem to discover a patriotic zeal nobody could imagine existed. The only other time I have seen it surface in this fashion was during the Falklands' crisis.

The Indians happened to be touring England then and some of them were surprised by what they saw as a reassertion of the old imperial lion. I must confess I was not entirely surprised since it seemed to me very evidently a working-out of an imperial nostalgia which has lain dormant since 1947 and the withdrawal from India. For many people this is still seen as a 'loss' – an unplanned and unnecessary defeat brought about by the conspiracy of foreigners and their collaborators in this country. I do not believe the British sought the Falklands war, nor do I share the Belgrano conspiracy theory. The war was forced upon Mrs Thatcher but she did understand the deep-seated British desire not to be pushed around any more. The memories of the shrinking red imperial colour on the map; India, Suez, Aden, Rhodesia, are still vivid in many minds and, as Mrs Thatcher said after the Falklands' victory 'it shows we can still do some of the things that made Britain great'. I am not saying, as Salman Rushdie seems to be, that the British still hanker after an empire or import immigrants into this country to indulge their empire fantasies. The British Empire was not all bad, as my father always maintained, but the point is that for many Britains the sudden change from the greatest power on earth to struggling European one is, I think, difficult to stomach. The Falklands provided an antidote and they eagerly welcomed it.

The war also brought home to me the gulf that fundamentally separates me from even my closest English friends. I was, I must confess, against the Falklands enterprise but though a good many of my English friends also felt the same way they could not but get emotionally involved with the tragedies and the successes that unfolded in the South Atlantic. I remember one night talking to my friend Bruce about this and saying, after the Argentinians had dropped a bomb which did not explode, 'you know you English are very lucky'. Bruce, who I had never suspected of any patriotism, fairly flared up. 'What do you mean lucky? Luck has nothing to do with it.' What I meant is that the British are unique among nations in having avoided being conquered for nearly one thousand years – not since the Normans. Look at any other country in Europe and you will see a cycle of conquest and liberation. France was under the German jackboot forty years ago, Russia still mourns her war dead and large parts of Asia, Africa and South America have been entirely remade by conquest. America has not been conquered but she is only two hundred years old.

I come from a country whose history is one of repeated conquests with supposedly superior Indian forces strangely unaccountably losing to marauding foreigners. I am no longer puzzled by it but it still pains me to read Indian history. It also gives me a certain perspective on the world, a certain way of looking at it which is different from how my English friends look at it. Some of my English friends occasionally interpret this as touchiness, a chip on the shoulder, when it really is a cry for understanding. My English friends can be sure about the world because they have made so much of it. I cannot because I do not quite know what world, if any, my ancestors have left for me.

It would be nice to say this book about Indian cricket is unique. I would like to think I have said things here that have not been said before – or at least not quite in this fashion. I have avoided the grand theory because while it is tempting to do so with India, this invariably makes one look stupid. I have refrained from predictions because everyone who writes anything about India loves to predict and, in my experience, most emerge with egg on their faces. You may like the country or hate it, but it has an infinite capacity for surprise.

I wrote this book because I wanted to share some of my love for Indian cricket which has often saddened me, every now and again infuriated me but provided rare moments of bliss surpassing almost everything. When I was young, Indian defeats would fill me with tears and in turn lead to fantasies of personal glorious deeds righting Indian cricket. Those glories never went beyond my bedroom mirror or the maidan game we played but in a way they were satisfying. Just as it was satisfying to try and imagine that I could bat like Tom Graveney and Mushtaq Ali, bowl fast like Lindwall and Miller and twirl my leg-spinners like Subhas Gupte. How I treasured Graveney's predictions in *Cricket Through the Covers* that on the 1959 Indian tour Gupte would be acclaimed as the great bowler, and how I raged when the task proved too much for him.

Even now I can barely contain myself when some ignorant English critic refuses to give Gupte his due as perhaps one of the finest postwar leg-spinners who was unfortunate enough to play in a team that could not catch – or often did not want to – and had no other bowlers. But then youthful fantasies are difficult to shake off.

Some years ago I caused a few comments in a journalists *Who's Who* by describing my fantasy of making a hundred at Lord's repeatedly hooking Trueman and Statham and powering India to a great win. As the Indians troop out to Lord's this summer I shall, for a fleeting moment, relive the fantasy – not so much scoring a hundred myself but imagining Indians winning the toss, batting, running up 600 for not much and then bowling out England twice by Saturday evening. Fantasies have a strange way of coming true. I doubt if any Indian could have imagined the circumstances of the Oval triumph of 1971 or the World cup win of 1983.

Just as the West Indies started their reply to India's 183 in that World cup final, I, tired of the rather rancid atmosphere of the Lord's press box, went for a walk. The Indians were depressed, the English and the Australians who had both been beaten by the

Indians made no secret of their contempt for the pathetic Indian showing – surely their own teams would have done better. As I neared the Tavern, Greenidge got out, soon after I returned to the press box, Richards was out, the rest is history.

It is part of the magic and mystery of sport that occasionally such fantasies come true. And when that happens what matters is not the wider meaning, whether it brings nations together or even creates a nation – as C. L. R. James thought of the West Indian tour of Australia in 1960–1 – but the joy it brings to those who have loved and followed the game, a joy like no other because it is sweet, unexpected and without any obligations.

I don't know, of course, what fantasies, if any, the Indians will fulfil this summer. Indian cricket has always seemed to be to me a bit like Gatsby in Scott Fitzgerald's *The Great Gatsby*. Having seen the green light at the end of Daisy's dock, 'He had come a long way to this blue lawn, and his dream must have seemed so close that he could hardly fail to grasp it.' But even as Gatsby grasped his dream it was behind him and to the Indian cricket follower 'the orgiastic future' recedes year by year. But like Scott Fitzgerald's narrator, the Indian cricket follower does believe that 'tomorrow we will run faster, stretch out our arms further ... And one fine morning –.'

INDEX

Acton, Lord
  Essay on Nationality 24
Adhukari, Hemu 163
Ahmad, Gulham 149
Akbar, M. J. 2–3, 10–11, 37
Alberuni, Muslim Scholar 4
Ali, Mohammed 3
Ali, Mushtaq 88, 174
Allenby, General 12
Amarnath, Lala 94
Amarnath, Mohinder 125
Amery, Leo
  Secretary of State for India 14
Amis, Kingsley 39
Amritraj, Vijay 157
Arlott, John 172
Arnold, Thomas 21–2, 24
Ashoka 3, 148
Ataturk, Kemal 48
Aurangzeb, Mughal Emperor 116
Ayer, A. J. 39
Azad Maidan, Bombay 78–9, 117
Azharuddin, Mohammad ('Azar') 2, 29, 70–1,
  124–5

Bahadur, Shah 9
Baig, Abbas Ali 141–3
Bailey, Trevor 16
Barlow, Richard 150
Barnett, Correlli 23, 25
Beaumont, Sir John – Chief Justice of Bombay
  High Court 95
Bedi, Bishan Singh 67, 122, 132, 134, 140–1,
  149, 151–2, 160–1
Bedser, Alec 153
Benaud, Richie 141
Berry, Scyld 15, 100, 165
Bharatan, Raju 137
Bhimani, Kishore 63
Bombay Cricket Association (BCA) 56–7, 121
Borde, Chandu 136–8, 140
Bose, Subhas 6, 10, 11, 25, 27, 30, 32, 35

Botham, Ian 60, 106, 127
Boycott, Geoff 60, 68, 122, 127, 135
Brabourne, Lord 56
Brabourne Stadium 44–5, 56, 121–2, 142
Bradman, Donald 89, 103, 109, 118–19, 132
Bragg, Melvyn 39
Brihaspati 3
Brittain-Jones, Major 93–4
Brockwell, W. 96

Cahn, Sir Julian 89
Cardus, Neville 38–9, 99, 155
Cashman, Dr Richard 39, 64, 86, 161
Chandrasekhar, Bhagwat 42, 70, 134, 149, 155,
  161–2
Chappell brothers 158
Chappell, Ian 20
Charter Act of 1813 26
Chaudhari, Vinay 108
Chaudhuri, Nirad 2, 4, 32, 128, 130, 148, 156–7
Clive, Robert 6–8, 26, 35, 61
Close, Brian 16
Clough, Brian 18
Columbus, Christopher 13
Compton, Denis 16
Contractor, Nari 133, 161
Cook, Geoff 68
Craddock, Sir Reginald 5
Cricket Association of Bengal 62
Cricket Club of India (CCI) 57–8, 121, 135
Cross Maidan, Bombay 78, 117
Crowe, Jeff 158
Crowe, Martin 158
Curzon, Lord 5

Daily Telegraph 17
Dalmiya, Jagmohan 62–3
Datta, Narendranath – *see* Swami
  Vivekananda
Delhi & District Cricket Association 58
de Mello, Anthony S. 95, 98–9, 168
Deodhar, Professor 137

176